Does God Hate Women?

Also available from Continuum:

Why Truth Matters, Ophelia Benson and Jeremy Stangroom

What Philosophers Think, edited by Julian Baggini and Jeremy Stangroom

What More Philosophers Think, edited by Julian Baggini and Jeremy Stangroom

Great Thinkers A–Z, edited by Julian Baggini and Jeremy Stangroom

Does **God Hate Women?**

Ophelia Benson and Jeremy Stangroom

continuum

Continuum
The Tower Building   80 Maiden Lane
11 York Road   Suite 704
London SE1 7NX   New York, NY 10038

www.continuumbooks.com

British Library Cataloguing-in-Publication Data
A catalogue record for this book is available from the British Library.

ISBN-10:   HB: 0-8264-9826-4
ISBN-13:   HB: 978-0-8264-9826-7

Library of Congress Cataloging-in-Publication Data
Benson, Ophelia.
    Does God hate women? / Ophelia Benson and Jeremy Strangroom.
        p.   cm.
    ISBN 978-0-8264-9826-7
  1. Women and religion.   I. Strangroom, Jeremy.   II. Title.

    BL458.B46 2009
    200.82–dc22   2008054792

Typeset by BookEns Ltd, Royston, Herts.
Printed and bound in Great Britain by MPG Books Ltd, Bodmin, Cornwall

Contents

Acknowledgements   vii

1   A God of Bullies   1

2   Religious Apologetics, Islam and Caricature   31

3   The World and the Kitchen   52

4   Honour Is Between the Legs of Women   83

5   Holy Groupthink   108

6   Mutilate in the Name of Purity   131

7   Islam, Islamophobia and Risk   151

8   Lipstick on a Pig   173

Notes   179

Index   199

For Gina Khan

Acknowledgements

The authors would like to thank Anthony Haynes and Sarah Campbell.

Additionally, Jeremy Stangroom would like to thank Charlotte Mirams and Cheryl O'Donoghue.

I will call no being good, who is not what I mean when I apply that epithet to my fellow-creatures; and if such a being can sentence me to hell for not so calling him, to hell I will go.

John Stuart Mill

1 A God of Bullies

They were punished for trying to decide for themselves about their marriages

In July 2008 five women were reportedly buried alive in Balochistan province, Pakistan. Three teenage girls attempted to marry men of their own choosing, against the wishes of tribal elders. They were kidnapped along with two older women who were accompanying them; all five were driven to a desert area by men belonging to the Umrani tribe, according to local reports. The three girls were beaten and shot and then thrown, still alive, into a ditch and covered with dirt and stones; when the other women protested they got the same treatment.[1]

The *Pakistan Tribune* reported that there seemed to be a consensus among tribal leaders on the issue:

> None of the leading Pashtoon or Baloch leaders have spoken a single critical word on this tragedy so far, as they prefer to respect the tribal decisions of killing their own women in the name of honour.[2]

In August, when details of the crime had begun to emerge, Senator Yasmeen Shah spoke in the Pakistani parliament to protest the murders. She was interrupted by Senator Israrullah Zehri from Balochistan, who said the killing or burial of women alive for 'honour' is a tribal tradition and should not be 'portrayed negatively'. He asked members not to politicize the issue, as it was a matter of safeguarding tribal traditions.[3]

In Lashkar Gah, Afghanistan, the majority of female prisoners are serving 20-year sentences for being raped. The system makes no distinction between women who have chosen to have sex with a man and women who have been raped: both are a crime that carries a maximum penalty of 20 years in prison. A high-ranking regional security officer, Colonel Ghulam Ali, told a reporter for the *Independent*, 'In Afghanistan whether it is forced or not forced it is a crime because the Islamic rules say that it is.'[4]

This is what makes religious law so oppressive: religious law is 'sacred' law and as such is above mere human needs and wishes. It is sacred and thus sacrosanct: fixed, peremptory and inviolate. It makes no difference how unjust and irrational it is to punish women for being raped; it is a crime because the Islamic rules say that it is.

She felt as though her insides were on fire

Ahmedi Begum, a 55-year-old widow in Lahore, Pakistan, needed to rent part of her house for income. Her daughter had just had her first baby and was still in bed and her son-in-law was at work when two young women, completely veiled, came to see the rooms that Begum wanted to rent. As Begum talked to them in the courtyard, several policemen burst in and arrested the young women along with Begum's nephew, who had just arrived. Later in the day, when Begum's son-in-law came home from work, the two of them went to the police station to ask what had happened.

The police put Begum in a separate room and told her they were arresting her too. She was shocked; she told them she was a respectable woman, a widow, a grandmother, that they were making a mistake, but they were unmoved. Then they brought in the two young women, naked and bleeding, and raped them again in front of her. She covered her eyes in anguish; the officers forced her to her knees and held her arms to her sides. 'Watch it! Watch it!' they shouted. Then they raped her too, one after another, over and over, all night. 'I don't know how many policemen came through that room that night. It could have been fifty. I will never forget their laughter, their shouting.'[5]

In the morning the policemen dragged her outside, held her face down, and beat her with a wide leather strap. The beating stopped suddenly – then she found herself screaming and screaming – she felt as though her insides were on fire. A policeman had shoved a truncheon covered with fiery chilli paste up her rectum with such force that her rectum was ruptured, and the chilli paste burned like acid.

Unconscious, she was put in Kot Lohkpat Women's Prison, charged with *zina*, adultery. (The two other women were charged with the crime of 'roaming about'.) Begum was in the prison for three months until the women's rights activist and lawyer Asma Jahangir got involved in her case. Three years later she was acquitted, but in the interval her son-in-law divorced her daughter because of the shame. Begum was left with a chronically ulcerated rectum and constant back pain from the beating. She thought the reason for her arrest was that she had recently refused to rent her spare rooms to a police officer.

The police tried to bribe Begum to drop her case against them. An official told her it would be bad for the police and for the country if the men were punished. Begum was unmoved, and the officers were charged, but they were never tried: they were transferred to different areas, as was the trial; the witnesses could not afford the travel expenses, and that was the end of that.[6]

Under Pakistan's Hudood Ordinance, introduced by General Zia ul Haq in 1979 as part of his programme of Islamization, a woman making an accusation of rape had to provide four Muslim men of good standing as witnesses to the crime. If she failed to provide such witnesses, the woman would be charged with *zina*, for which the prescribed punishment was flogging or stoning, though such punishments were never actually carried out in Pakistan.[7] According to Human Rights Watch, however, thousands of women were imprisoned as a result of unsuccessful charges of rape.[8] The result was that rape could be committed with impunity in Pakistan.

In 2002 Zafran Bibi, a peasant woman from Northwest Frontier Province, said that her husband's brother had repeatedly raped her. Her husband was in prison for murder and in his absence she became a toy for at least one of his brothers. The attacks came sometimes on the hillside behind her house when she went to cut hay, sometimes at home when no one was around. Her lawyer said she complained to her mother-in-law and father-in-law but they paid no attention. But she became pregnant, and that forced her accusations into the open. The result was that she was convicted of *zina*.

The judge who convicted her, Anwar Ali Khan, said he had simply followed the letter of the Hudood Ordinance. 'The illegitimate child is not disowned by her and therefore is proof of *zina*,' he said; furthermore, in accusing her brother-in-law of raping her, Zafran had confessed to her crime. 'The lady stated before this court that, yes, she had committed sexual intercourse, but with the brother of her husband,' Judge Khan said. 'This left no option to the court but to impose the highest penalty.' Zafran's brother-in-law, Jamal Khan, was released without charge. 'With the men, they apply the principle that you are innocent until proven guilty,' Asma Jahangir told a *New York Times* reporter. 'With the women, they apply the principle that you are guilty until proven innocent.'

The reporter visited Zafran's parents, who had rarely seen her after she was given in marriage to Niamat Khan; they are too poor even to have a photograph of her.

> They sat silently one recent day on the string beds that are the only furnishings of their bare one-room home.
>
> Ms. Zafran's father, Zaidan, an unsmiling, weatherbeaten man, spread his hands as if he had no words to offer.
>
> 'When we heard the sentence, we couldn't breathe,' he said at last. 'We couldn't think. For days we couldn't eat. There was nothing we could do for our daughter.' He said he had sold his family's only possessions, two thin goats, to help pay for a lawyer.

His wife, Shiraka, whose beauty seems only to have been deepened by her difficult life, looked away. 'I have been sucked dry by grief,' she said.[9]

In spite of strong opposition from religious groups, Musharraf's government passed the Protection of Women Bill in December 2006; the bill placed rape laws under the penal code and did away with 'harsh conditions that previously required victims to produce four male witnesses and exposed them to prosecution for adultery if they were unable to prove the crime'.[10] Religious groups held protests throughout the country when the bill was passed.

We are just complying with the laws of Allah, so we don't have anything to worry about

In September 2000 Bariya Ibrahim Magazu was sentenced by an Islamic Court in the Nigerian state of Zamfara to a flogging sentence of 180 lashes with a cane. Magazu was unsure of her age but thought she was 13 or 14; the judge said as long as she has started menstruating she is considered a full and responsible adult. Magazu was pregnant and unmarried, so she was charged with *zina*. At her trial she said she was pressured into having sex with three married men from her village. There were unconfirmed reports that her father owed the three men money and that sex with Bariya was a way to pay off the debt.

Bariya Magazu called seven witnesses, but the men were acquitted because the witnesses' testimony was judged insufficient to prove they had had intercourse with her. Sharia (Islamic law) requires that at least four witnesses of good character testify that 'not a hair could pass between their bodies'.[11] Magazu was sentenced to 100 lashes for *zina* and, because the men were acquitted, another 80 lashes for *qadhf*, false accusation of *zina*. A women's rights group went to the governor of Zamfara to request leniency, but he said no on the grounds that this would be detrimental to Islam. He also dismissed letters and protests from human rights groups because the groups are not Muslim or based on Muslim laws, and thus unqualified to comment.[12] In January 2001, a court reduced the sentence to 100 lashes; while an appeal of the case and the sentence as a whole was still pending, officials carried out the whipping on 19 January 2001.[13]

New Sharia penal codes came into force in 12 states in northern Nigeria starting in 1999; under these codes *zina* carries a mandatory death sentence if the accused is married, while 100 lashes is the mandatory sentence if the accused is not married. The charge of *zina* and the punishment for it prescribed in law applies to Muslims only. The application of the death penalty for *zina* offences combined with the discriminatory evidence rules within *Sharia* penal codes have meant that women have disproportionately been sentenced to death for *zina* in northern Nigeria since the introduction of the new penal codes.[14]

In Sokoto a court convicted Safiya Hussaini of adultery and sentenced her to death by stoning because she became pregnant out of wedlock, even though the mother of five said she was raped by a neighbour, Yakubu Abubakar. He too was charged with adultery, but was acquitted by the Sharia court that convicted Safiya. He had confessed to her family, in the presence of two police officers, but he retracted his confession in court; he claimed that he had never met Safiya, even though they lived in the same tiny village. Under Sharia, if a man withdraws his confession, he must be acquitted, unless four men testify that they witnessed the adulterous act. A woman does not have that option: if she becomes pregnant outside marriage, that is all the evidence required. Safiya's lawyer did not request that Yakubu appear in the appeal court to answer the rape charge. 'He has been acquitted, why should he be made to suffer again?' the lawyer asked Dan Isaacs of the BBC. Aliyu Abubakar Sanyinna is the Sokoto state attorney general. He told Isaacs, 'It is the law of Allah. By executing anybody that is convicted under Islamic law, we are just complying with the laws of Allah, so we don't have anything to worry about.'[15]

Safiya's conviction was overturned in March 2002, just as Amina Lawal Kurami was sentenced to death by stoning for bearing a child more than nine months after she was divorced. She said the man who fathered her child had promised to marry her, but he said he was not the father and three male witnesses testified that he had not had a sexual relationship with Lawal. The witnesses constituted adequate corroboration of his story under Sharia law, and he was freed. As a result of international outrage, Lawal's conviction was overturned in February 2004.[16]

A crusade against 'unchaste' behaviour

In Jerusalem in June 2008 a young divorced woman was reportedly beaten by a group of ultra-Orthodox young men who entered her apartment and demanded that she move out because she had been seen in the company of married men. When she refused, three of the men allegedly attacked her, knocking her to the floor and kicking her. They warned her she would be blinded with mace and stabbed if she dared to open her eyes. She was then 'interrogated' by the gang as they tried to force her to disclose the identities of men she had been in contact with.

The men were members of the 'tznius patrol' or modesty police. In August a 28-year-old Jerusalem man, Elhanan Buzaglo, was charged with the attack; a number of other women have filed complaints about him for incidents ranging from verbal harassment to attempting to run over a girl with a car.[17] Also in June, a 14-year-old girl in Betar Illit had acid spilled on her face and body; the incident was attributed to another modesty patrol in the town. The indictment charges that the modesty patrol has declared a crusade against violations of Halachic law and what it views as 'unchas behaviour, using intimidation and violence as the means to end.[18] The patrol seems to attack only women.

A woman was beaten by what *Ha'aretz* called 'an ad hoc n

patrol' on a Jerusalem bus in 2006. A group of Haredi (ultra-Orthodox) men had demanded that she move to the back of the bus with the other women; she had refused, and the men slapped, kicked, punched and pushed her. 'Every two or three days, someone would tell me to sit in the back, sometimes politely and sometimes not,' she told *Ha'aretz* in an interview. 'I was always polite and said "No". This is not a synagogue. I am not going to sit in the back.' Then one day the man who told her to move did not accept her refusal but said 'I'm not asking you, I'm telling you'; he assaulted her, and other men joined in.[19]

It was a disgusting experience, so degrading

'Faribah', a 55-year-old woman in Tehran, had been shopping at a supermarket and was about to put her bags of groceries in her car when she was arrested. She was baffled at first but then realized her headscarf had slipped back from her forehead a little; because her arms were full of groceries she hadn't been able to pull it back into place. More than a hundred women were arrested with her. At Monkarat jail she was told her crime was that her hair was showing and the split at the back of her long coat (to make walking possible) was too high, though she was wearing trousers underneath.

The punishment for bad hijab is one to twelve months in prison or whipping or both. Sometimes a fine can substitute for the whipping; 80 lashes could cost between six and twelve months' average income. Faribah was kept in jail for seven hours, until her husband put up the deed of their house as bail. When she went to trial she was sentenced to 80 lashes. With other women arrested at the same time, she was taken to the basement of the building.

Two *Pasdaran* took me into a cell, one holding a whip in his hand. They handcuffed me facedown on a wooden bed. All I could think was, 'This is not really happening, this is not Islamic, how can a religious government men do this to women?' Then they started whipping me.[20]

She thinks the whipping hurt her mentally more than physically. 'I was so shocked that this was happening. It was the total helplessness and subjugation, the lack of power, being robbed of all dignity. It was a disgusting experience, so degrading, and as violating in its way as rape.' It also made her realize what the Iranian regime thinks of women.[21]

Pakistan, Zamfara, Afghanistan, Iran are all officially Islamic states, all avowedly polities in which religion and government are thoroughly intertwined. It is interesting to note that this interaction seems to result in a ferociously punitive and brutal regime for women, a regime in which they are whipped, gang-raped, tortured, for not much more than being women. A hundred lashes for a 14-year-old girl for what in other legal systems would be statutory rape even if she had consented; 80 lashes for a 55-year-old woman because her hijab revealed a little hair while she was laden with groceries; gang-rape, beating and torture for a 55-year-old woman for ... nothing. What is the connection between the intertwinement of religion and the state, and this sort of treatment? Why *does* this interaction issue in such savagery toward women?

Barnaby Rogerson said recently, in a *Times Literary Supplement* review of Tariq Ramadan's *The Messenger: The Meanings of the Life of Muhammad*, that Ramadan does not 'lose sight of the animating purpose of true religion, to charge mankind with love and compassion, and subdue the brutal realities of the competitive hunger which we all share'.[22] If the animating purpose of true religion is to charge human beings with love and compassion, why do we find that the most strenuously and conspicuously 'devout' countries have such punitive laws and customs? Why is it the *religious* police who arrest a woman with her arms full of bags of groceries for having allowed her hijab to slip? Why do the laws of highly religious Iran punish an inch of visible hair with 80 lashes? Where, exactly, are the love and compassion there? Clearly not in the punishment of th perpetrator, so is it perhaps for the victims of her crime? The pec harmed by the sight of a woman's hair? The question answers

Where, then? Where is the compassion in the sentence of 160 lashes given to the victim of a gang rape? If the animating purpose of true religion is to charge human beings with love and compassion, why was the Taliban's very first act on seizing Kabul to issue decrees imprisoning women and forbidding them to do almost everything? Not charity, not caring for the poor, not tending to the sick and injured, not mutual aid, but telling women to stop working, stop learning, stop going outside.

Humans are moderately sexually dimorphic – less so than gorillas, more so than gibbons; roughly comparable to chimpanzees. Human males are on average larger and stronger than human females. That fact by itself is enough to explain why throughout recorded history women have been subordinate to men and why in most of the world they still are. Men dominate women because they can.

There are of course other reasons and explanations, of which more later. But one human institution that has always cast its lot with the stronger side – that has strengthened the arm of the already strong, added its weight to the already heavy, given the halo of sanctity to the existing power imbalance – that has for millennia helped the stronger to go on dominating the weaker – is religion.

This is interesting because religion is widely supposed to be centrally about compassion, justice, mercy – qualities not usually attributed to enforcing the subordination of the underdog. It can be tempting to conclude that compassion and justice are simply labels attached to whatever religion does, to make its votaries feel good, rather than descriptions of reality.

However that may be, the reality is that religion is very often somewhere on the scene when women are being regulated, or punished, or deprived, or coerced. What would otherwise look like stark bullying is very often made respectable and holy by a putative religious law or aphorism or scriptural quotation. The case of Ahmedi Begum and her two prospective lodgers looks on the face of it like one sort of opportunistic sex crime, a story for *Law and Order SVU*, Pakistan's Hudood Ordinances lurk in the background.

Religion dresses up power in robes and mitres; it disguises *force majeure* as the will of a male God. This makes everyone feel better. Men are doing what God wants them to do, and so are women. Women have narrow confined restricted lives and no right to their own will because that is what God ordained.

I would love to send Adijah to school, but I really need her to work

When something goes wrong in northern Ghana, one remedy is to charge a woman with witchcraft. During an outbreak of meningitis in 1997, two elderly women in the northern district of Kumbugu were beaten to death by the people who accused them of causing the disease.[23] Hundreds of women have fled from home after being charged with witchcraft, going to special villages which are refuges but also prisons. The women are free to leave, but they have nowhere else to go.

> Near death after a 30-mile, weeklong walk, Tarana says she arrived at the Gambaga camp, which has sheltered accused witches since the late eighteenth century. Chief Ganbaraaba, she says, took her in, had her wounds tended to, and sent for Tarana's children.
> Not one has come.[24]

The daughters of refugees sometimes spend months at the camps to help their mothers, but more often they send a daughter of their own to do chores.

> While Adijah Iddrissu's doll-like hands busy themselves shelling groundnuts, her large piercing eyes track her grandmother.
> At 7, Adijah already has put in a year at Kpatinga …
> Iddrissu explains: 'I would love to send Adijah to school, but I really need her to work.'
> Fifteen of the 45 outcasts at Kpatinga have a granddaughter with
> Like Adijah, none goes to school. What's worse, many of the girls

slide back into their communities after their grandmothers die. To do so means being stigmatized possibly stoned – as punishment for associating with a witch.

They, too, will live out their lives in exile.[25]

Her face was bruised and bloated from beatings

At a public meeting in a village in the Indian state of Jharkhand, men gathered for a public meeting. A fragile young woman was dragged in by two men.

> Her face was bruised and bloated from beatings; she had been dragged stark naked through the village the previous evening. Even from a distance I could see the welt marks where the sticks had fallen mercilessly on her slender frame … Tears, blood and mucus had dried on her face and she looked lifeless.
>
> Two men of the village threw the woman like a bundle of rags in the middle of the gathering. 'This woman is a witch!' the two men announced to the villagers … One or two young boys poked her with twigs, spitting and demanding she show her powers to the multitude. 'Hey Dyan (witch), get up, get up. Show us what you can do!' they shouted over and over again.

Two men held Budhaniya Majhi roughly by her feet and hands while a third, ignoring her screams and pleas, poured a cup of cow urine down her throat. She gagged. The village council sentenced her to leave the village, giving her house, land and animals – a cow and two goats – to her brother-in-law as compensation for killing his father with witchcraft. She and her month-old baby were destitute and had nowhere to go.[26]

You have grown old. Now who is going to feed you?

Widows in India are faced with both destitution and social abandonment. They are considered bad luck or inauspicious as well as a financial burden, and the result often is that they are ostracized and shunned. 'Women get up first, sleep last, eat least, work twenty-four hours, and are not recognized at all,' says Dr V. Mohini Giri, founder of the War Widows Association.[27]

In traditional Hindu society a widowed woman is expected either to commit suicide in order to keep her husband company or to go into an *ashram* to live alone for the rest of her life. She is considered inauspicious and therefore avoided.[28]

Sati is illegal in modern India, as is its 'glorification', but widows still undergo ritual humiliations after their husbands die. The widow is stripped of her bridal ornaments, her head is shaved by a barber, and she puts on a plain white sari so that she will not arouse other men. The *sindoor*, the red smear that a married woman wears at her hairline, is exchanged for a vertical ash smear from the top of her forehead to the top of her nose. Her presence is considered so inauspicious that even her shadow may not fall on a married woman.[29] Many Hindu widows go to the city of Vrindavan to wait to die. They are not allowed to remarry, they must not wear jewelry, they are destitute.

The widows have to sing prayers in two four-hour shifts, morning and afternoon, to earn a daily five rupees and a handful of rice.[30]

'Does it feel good?' says 70-year-old Rada Rani Biswas. 'Now I have to loiter just for a bite to eat.'

Biswas speaks with a strong voice, but her spirit is broken. When her husband of 50 years died, she was instantly ostracized by all those she thought loved her, including her son.

'My son tells me: "You have grown old. Now who is going to feed you. Go away," ' she says, her eyes filling with tears. 'What do I do? My pain no limit.'

As she speaks, she squats in front of one of Vrindavan's temples, her life reduced to begging for scraps of food.[31]

Giri tells the story of Shanta Bai. She was married when she was 5 years old; her uncle received Rs.300 for marrying her to a 36-year-old man. The husband died four years later, leaving Bai a 9-year-old widow. She is now 85, living in Vrindavan, holding a broken begging bowl while she waits for her life to end.[32]

The BBC's Jill McGivering visited Vrindavan in 2002.

The women line up, after singing for several hours, to receive a cup of rice and a few teaspoons of lentils. It isn't much ... We met Nirmala Dasi, a frail 85-year-old, begging at the temple gate. When she spoke, she dissolved into tears.

'I've been too ill to sing at the temple for the last three days so I haven't had a thing to eat. You don't get anything unless you go there.'[33]

McGivering soon found herself surrounded by widows with sad stories to tell.

'I spend almost everything I get on a room I share with four others. I've no relatives, or I wouldn't be here,' said Mithila.

'It's so cold here, I'm always freezing.'[34]

She would have run away, just like Fauziya, if she had been old enough

In Togo, Hajia Kassindja's elder sister died as a result of female genital mutilation, which led Hajia's parents to spare her from the practice. Her husband Muhammad could remember the screams of his own sister during her FGM, and the suffering she endured from a tetanus infection afterwards. The pair had five daughters and two sons, and they did not have any of their daughters cut. They also sent all their daughters to school. The four elder daughters grew up and married men of their own choosing, as their mother had; the youngest daughter, Fauziya, was 15 when her father died suddenly, and everything changed. As is the custom in Togo, Fauziya's father's relatives took possession of his property and turned her mother out of the house. The father's widowed sister moved in and took over Fauziya's upbringing. Two years before Fauziya was to graduate, the aunt – herself illiterate – took Fauziya out of school. She later told *New York Times* reporter Celia Dugger, 'We don't want girls to go to school too much. We don't think girls should be too civilized.'[35]

The aunt and the family patriarch – a cousin of Muhammad Kassindja – also arranged Fauziya's marriage to a man who had three wives already and wanted Fauziya for the fourth. His wives all had had FGM and he wanted Fauziya to have it too; the aunt and the patriarch agreed.

> Mrs. Mamoude said that she could tell Fauziya did not want to marry or be cut, though the young woman did not openly refuse. But Fauziya said she pleaded all summer with her aunt not to make her marry Mr. Ibrahim. Her aunt was angered and stopped calling her by name, Fauziya said, referring to her only as 'Hey you, who has no respect.'[36]

Fauziya's mother had $3,500 that her husband's family had allowed her from his property; she gave $3,000 to Fauziya to enable her to flee the country. Fauziya refused to sign a marriage certificate that the groom had sent to her; the next day her sister arrived to help her run away. The women who were to hold her down and cut off her genitals were already in the house, talking to her aunt in a back room. The sisters walked out of the house; they took a taxi to Ghana, 20 miles away, then another to the airport in Accra. Fauziya flew to Germany, then to the USA, where she had relatives. When she arrived in Newark she asked for asylum, and was taken to an immigration detention center. She was detained for more than a year, but in June 1996 the Board of Immigration Appeals granted her asylum; the decision was the Board's first recognition of genital mutilation as a form of persecution and a basis for asylum, and set a binding precedent for the 179 other immigration judges in the USA.[37]

Celia Dugger talked to the patriarch, Mouhamadou Kassindja, about FGM in the aftermath of the decision.

> He said genital cutting was done because his forefathers had done it. Women who were not cut would be mocked. The rite was not required by Islam, he said, but neither did the prophet Mohammed forbid it.[38]

His youngest wife was cut when she married him at the age of 15; she said the agony of having her genitals cut off with a razor blade was far worse than childbirth, but she nevertheless approves of the practice because it reveals virginity. Another wife, Salamatou, said she would have run away, just like Fauziya, if she had been old enough.

> She remembered a woman sitting on her chest when she was a little girl as others held her legs apart while her clitoris and genital lips were cut off
> …
>   'I have to do what my husband says,' she said. 'It is not for women to give an order. I feel what happened to my body. I remember my suffering, but I cannot prevent it for my daughter.'
>   Later, in her small, cell-like bedroom, she spread Fatima's pudgy thighs apart, then made a quick scooping motion with her hand to show that all the delicate tissue there would be cut away.[39]

Life for women under the Taliban was no more than being cows in sheds

Safia Amajan risked torture, imprisonment and death under the Taliban by secretly studying literature and writing poetry. Her first book – *Gul-e-dodi* (Dark Red Flower) – was widely praised; she was working on her second book; then in November 2005 she was beaten to death.

> Friends say her family was furious, believing that the publication of poetry by a woman about love and beauty had brought shame on it.
>   'She was a great poet and intellectual but, like so many Afghan women,

she had to follow orders from her husband,' said Nahid Baqi, her best friend at Herat University.[40]

Her husband was arrested after confessing to having slapped her during a quarrel, but he denied killing her and claimed that Amajan committed suicide.

She was one of the group of women known as the Sewing Circles of Herat, who risked their lives to keep the city's literary scene active under the Taliban. Women were banned from working or studying; the Taliban forbade women to laugh aloud or wear shoes that clicked. Women in Herat's Literary Circle realized that one of the few things that women were still permitted to do was sew, so three times a week groups of women in burqas would arrive at the Golden Needle Sewing School. No one did any sewing there; instead the women discussed Shakespeare, Dostoevsky and other banned writers with a professor of literature from Herat University. In a world where teaching a daughter to read was a crime, they could have been hanged if they had been caught.

Christina Lamb, author of *The Sewing Circles of Herat*, described the school in *The Times* shortly after Amajan's murder.

> I was taken to meet some of these women by Ahmed Said Haghighi, president of the Literary Circle, in December 2001, only days after the Taliban had fled. One of them, Leila, said that she stayed up till the early hours doing calculus because she so feared that her brain would atrophy. 'Life for women under the Taliban was no more than being cows in sheds,' she said.[41]

The resurgent Taliban succeeded in shutting down schools in Afghanistan in 2005 and 2006. Schools for girls were hit particularly hard.

> Human Rights Watch found entire districts in Afghanistan where attacks had closed all schools and driven out the teachers and non-governmental organizations providing education. Insecurity, societal resistance in some quarters to equal access to education for girls, and a lack of resources mean that, despite advances in recent years, the majority of girls in the

country remain out of school. Nearly one-third of districts have no girls' schools.[42]

Societal resistance plays itself out as forced marriage of young girls for the most frivolous of reasons.

In Afghanistan a 12-year-old girl named Shabana was forced to marry a man 38 years her senior to settle her father's $600 gambling debt in 2005. She is unhappy and angry; she doesn't like her husband, she doesn't get along with his first wife, and she is disgusted with her father. 'He sold me,' she told Shoib Najafizada of Agence France Presse in 2007. Shabana was taken out of school to marry 52-year-old farmer Mohammad Asef.

'He is wild – he destroyed my hopes,' she said in their humble mudbrick home in the northern province of Balkh, speaking out only when Asef went into another room to take a call. [S]he spends most of her time doing chores in the simple house.[43]

Human Rights Watch provided testimony from many individuals:

'In the first three years there were a lot of girl students – everyone wanted to send their daughters to school. For example, in Argandob district, girls were ready; women teachers were ready. But when two or three schools were burned, then nobody wanted to send their girls to school after that.'

'The Taliban went to each class, took out their long knives ... locked the children in two rooms, [where they] were severely beaten with sticks and asked, "will you come to school now?" The teachers said that they were taken out of school. The Taliban asked them individually, "Why are you working for Bush and Karzai?" They said, "We are educating our children with books – we know nothing about Bush or Karzai, we are just educating our children." After that, they were cruelly beaten and let go.'

'I saw these two men ... One of them fired a full magazine in Laghmani's chest ... I was afraid for my life and hid around a corner. I did not know who the victim was. After the killers fled, I went to the gate and saw Laghmani lying dead ... It was awful ... We have been receiving night letters, but no one thought they would really kill a teacher!'

'After reading this letter, I along with my family decided not to go to school because those who are warning us are quite powerful and strong. We are ordinary people and we can not challenge them. Also, I asked the girls from my village not to go back to school ... All the girls from my village would really like to attend that school ... but the problem is security – what will happen if they really plant bombs on our way? That's the reason.'[44]

Generations of women had sacrificed their feelings to preserve the work of God

Carolyn Jessop was born into the Fundamentalist Church of Jesus Christ of Latter-Day Saints, a Mormon offshoot that still practises polygamy, or, as they call it, 'plural marriage'. Her grandmother taught her she had been blessed 'to come into a family where generations of women had sacrificed their feelings to preserve the work of God'. Her only purpose was to have as many children as possible. This did not explain why her mother beat her so often or why so many of the women wore dark glasses to hide their black eyes, but it did give her a feeling of having been singled out for something important.

Jessop was 18 when her father announced that God had picked a husband for her: Merril Jessop, a 50-year-old man with weathered skin and yellow teeth. She had never met him, but she knew he already had three wives and several dozen children. She had gone to school with some of his daughters. She had heard bad things about the way Merril treated his family. Boys who worked for his construction company said he didn't pay them and he worked them like dogs.

She adored her father, and her church had taught her 'to honour our mothers and our father', but she was outraged. Her father, however, explained that when a directive like this came down from the Prophet, it was essential not to waste time.

I could barely breathe – then Dad said the wedding would take place in two days' time. My life had been swiped out from under me.

I later discovered that Merril had married into my family only to stop my father suing him over a business deal that had gone sour. More humiliating still, he hadn't meant to marry me, but my younger and prettier sister, Annette. When he asked the Prophet to arrange the marriage, Merril got our names mixed up.[45]

Afghanistan, Arizona – they're not as different as one might expect. Carolyn Jessop was allowed to stay in school longer than Shabana, but she was handed over to a stranger just as peremptorily as Shabana was. In secular society, forcing girls to have sex with unknown men is called pimping, and it is straightforwardly a crime. If it's done under the umbrella of religion, and the girl is handed over for marriage rather than prostitution, then it is no longer a crime. But from the point of view of the girl, the experience is much the same – she is forced to have sex with a stranger. She also has no ability to decide the shape of her life for herself; she is an object of exchange between men, handed over like furniture or farm equipment.

Child marriage and early childbirth can cause physical damage to girls. In particular it can cause fistula, a hole in the wall between the vagina and the bladder or rectum. Every year from 50,000 to 100,000 women giving birth in poor countries are left with this affliction,[46] which renders them incontinent, wet, smelly and ostracized. Child marriage is one of those practices that are part religion, part custom, and that, whatever the causal proportions are, religion makes much harder to reform.

The BBC spoke to one such woman during an international conference on maternal health in October 2007. Halima Gouroukoye of Niamey, Niger, was 13 when her parents arranged her marriage; she wasn't happy about it but they told her the prospective husband was a good man and would look after her. She got pregnant after her first period and gave birth at 14. She was ill throughout her pregnancy, but she still had to do all her usual work – collect wood, prepare meals, clean the house and care for her husband as well as work in the fields. She was in labour for two days at home, then went to a clinic, where she was told she would need a Caesarean.

> [B]ut the doctor sent me home because I couldn't afford the operation.
>
> I had to wait for my family to collect the money to pay for the operation. Then we drove to Niamey which took a day. By that stage I had been in labour for days. I didn't know where I was, I was almost unconscious.[47]

The baby died, and three days later Halima realized she couldn't hold her urine. She didn't tell her husband, but went home to her parents. Everyone thought she was cursed. Two months later she returned to Niamey, where an NGO provided her with the operation to mend the fistula.

Dr Kees Waaldijk runs a clinic for fistula patients in Katsina, Nigeria. He has operated on 15,000 fistulas in 22 years, repairing nearly all of them.

> Safiya, 23, was in the post-op ward after living for a year in the hut of a traditional healer who tried to cure her by stuffing potions into her vagina. Daso, 23, said she had leaked urine and feces for five years. Her husband divorced her.
>
> Rumasau, 16, unluckily began labor on a Saturday, when her local hospital had no physician for her. She had to wait until the following Tuesday for an emergency Caesarean section.[48]

The operation is simple and nearly always successful, but the number of new cases is far outpacing repairs, and many girls are repaired simply to be re-broken. 'To be a woman in Africa is truly a terrible thing,' Dr Waaldijk observed.[49]

But not only in Africa.

Mami, they are not treating me

Abortion is tightly restricted in several South American countries. Colombia used to have a total ban, until its Constitutional Court ruled on 10 May 2006 that abortion in cases of rape, foetal malformation and endangerment of the life of the mother should be legal. The lawsuit was brought before the court by Monica Roa of Women's Link Worldwide, who was the target of death threats, burglaries, and charges of genocide in the course of her effort. Her opponents were senior figures within the Church, who are enormously powerful in a country where more than 90 per cent of the population is Catholic.[50]

Nicaragua redressed the balance by enacting its own blanket ban in November 2006, joining Chile and El Salvador as the three countries in the world to have such total bans. The law was ratified by the National Assembly in September 2007. Both the original enactment and the vote in September 2007 were widely attributed to the desire of political parties to ensure and maintain support from the Roman Catholic Church and the Evangelical Church. Human Rights Watch issued a report in October that year on the serious effects the ban was having on the lives and health of women and girls. HRW found no prosecutions of doctors under the new law, yet also that 'the mere possibility of facing criminal charges for providing lifesaving health services has had a deadly effect'.[51]

> Sofía M.'s doctor told Human Rights Watch she had been diagnosed years earlier with a mental imbalance that causes her to be violent whenever she is not medicated. In March 2007, when she discovered she was pregnant, Sofía M. knew she could not carry the pregnancy to term. She said, 'I don't want to kill. But in my case, I couldn't have the child … It would not be born healthy because I can't stop taking the medicine … If I can't even take care of me, how would I take care of a child?'
>
> Sofía M. and her mother went from one clinic to another, but no one wanted to carry out the abortion because of the law: 'They said they couldn't do it because it is illegal.' She finally found a clandestine provider through a friend and told Human Rights Watch of the added anxiety in having to procure illegal services: 'I was afraid; I did not know what it was going to be like.'[52]

Others were not so lucky.

Angela M.'s 22-year-old daughter is another case in point. Her pregnancy-related hemorrhaging was left untreated for days at a public hospital in Managua, despite the obligation, even under Nicaraguan law and guidelines, to treat such life-threatening emergencies. In November 2006, only days after the blanket ban on abortion was implemented, Angela M. told Human Rights Watch of the pronounced lack of attention: 'She was bleeding ... That's why I took her to the emergency room ... but the doctors said that she didn't have anything ... Then she felt worse [with fever and hemorrhaging] and on Tuesday they admitted her. They put her on an IV and her blood pressure was low ... She said, "Mami, they are not treating me.".…They didn't treat at all, nothing.'

From comments made by the doctors at the time, Angela M. believes her daughter was left untreated because doctors were reluctant to treat a pregnancy-related emergency for fear that they might be accused of providing therapeutic abortion. Angela M.'s daughter was finally transferred to another public hospital in Managua, but too late: 'She died of cardiac arrest ... She was all purple, unrecognizable. It was like it wasn't my daughter at all.'[53]

Chile's 1874 penal code made abortion illegal in all cases; in 1931 a national health law allowed doctors to give legal abortions where necessary to save the pregnant woman's life or health. In 1989 General Pinochet, as one of his last acts in office, annulled this statutory exception to the general illegality of abortion; thus the law now prohibits abortion in all circumstances. Nevertheless, a very large number of women risk illegal and thus unsafe abortions every year; surveys indicate that 35 per cent of all pregnancies in Chile end in abortion, which translates to about 160,000 abortions per year, 64,000 of them by girls under 18. Illegal abortion is a leading cause of maternal mortality in Chile.[54]

In Lublin, Poland, a 14-year-old schoolgirl known by the pseudonym 'Agata' said she was raped by a fellow student and left covered in bruises and pregnant. She and her mother applied for permission to have an abortion, which in Poland is legal up to 12 weeks in cases of rape, but when they went to the hospital, Agata was shown, alone, into a room where a priest was waiting. The doctor returned later and said she would not perform the abortion; Agata says the doctor and the priest dictated a letter in which she agreed to keep the baby, and she complied just to get some peace. Her mother contacted the Women's Federation in Warsaw and, with their help, found a clinic willing to perform the abortion, but when they arrived they found the same priest waiting, along with anti-abortion campaigners; the doctors then refused to perform the abortion. Agata told the *Gazeta Wyborcza* that she wants to be a mother later, not now.[55]

We have our own package of values

In August 2000 Muslim women in the northern Nigerian state of Zamfara were banned from riding on motorbikes. Authorities who enacted the law said it was a 'safety measure' in response to the high number of motorbike accidents involving women and children. The BBC's correspondent in Zamfara reported that after the ban only men and non-Muslim women were allowed to ride on motorbikes in the capital, Gusau. The council said it would punish anyone caught disobeying the law: imprisonment for three months, twenty strokes of the cane, and confiscation of the motorbike for three weeks.[56]

In May 2007 the newspaper *Iran* reported plans to make 'Islamic bicycles' for women that would conceal the movements of their bodies while riding. The bicycle would have a cabin that would cover half the woman's body, according to project manager Elaheh Sofali.

Iran's conservative clerics have blocked repeated efforts of reformers and feminists to promote athletics for women. Female athletes are forced to wear the same scarves and long gowns for sport that they are required to wear in the street and other public spaces. The clergy considers women's body movements made while riding a bicycle to be provoking to men.[57]

In Gujranwala, Pakistan in April 2005 a mob of men wielding sticks flung petrol bombs and set fire to vehicles at a mini-marathon which included women. The threat of more violence forced the cancellation of other mini-marathons scheduled that week. The race was attacked by supporters of Muttahida Majlis-e-Amal, an alliance of Islamic political parties.

> 'Marathons are not objectionable – as long as the menfolk and womenfolk run separately,' said Syed Munawar Hassan, a senior MMA leader. 'Every society is not an American or western society. We have our own package of values.'[58]

My sister wanted to run away from the house and was stopped

Banaz Mahmod was born in the Kurdish region of Iraq; her family fled to London when she was 10. Her father, Mahmod Mahmod, was a strict Muslim and ruled his six children 'with a rod of iron'.

> When Bekhal, an older sister, wore Western dress her father called her a whore, beat her and demanded that she wear the veil. She eventually went into foster care and, when old enough, severed all links with the family.[59]

When Banaz was 17 she was married to a man in his thirties from Iraq. The marriage was miserable. One day when one of her sisters noticed she was covered in bruises, Banaz said she had slipped in the bath; that's what her husband had told her to say. She once called him by his first name in front of his friends; he punched her and knocked out a tooth, for being disrespectful. She eventually left him and returned to live with her parents; then she met another man and began seeing him in secret. Her father Mahmod discovered the relationship in October 2005. Banaz's cousin Ala overheard her father discussing the need to kill Banaz with Banaz's father and other male relatives; Ala warned Banaz, and Banaz told the police. On New Year's Eve Banaz's father took her to her grandmother's house, put on surgical gloves, and gave her alcohol to drink; she ran away in terror, breaking a neighbour's window with her bare hands to get attention and then collapsing in the street. She was taken to the hospital, where her boyfriend recorded her on video describing what had happened. After she recovered she returned home, telling the police that she would be okay because her mother would be there to protect her. On 24 January 2006 her parents left the house, then her father returned with several other men and killed her. They removed her body in a suitcase, which they buried in a garden in Birmingham.[60]

Samaira Nazir wanted to marry her longstanding Afghan boyfriend Salman Mohammed rather than any of the men in Pakistan her family wanted her to marry. Nazir was 25, and said to be 'strong-willed'; she ran a recruitment agency in Southall, bordering London. When she rejected all her suitors in Pakistan, she was summoned to the family home in Southall. There her elder brother and a teenage cousin stabbed her repeatedly and then cut her throat. They forced the brother's two daughters, aged 4 and 2, to watch. Neighbours called the police when they heard Samaira scream; the brother, Azhar Nazir, explained to the officers: 'She does not wish to have an arranged marriage. We only allow marriage within the family. My sister wanted to run away from the house and was stopped.'[61]

Hatun Sürücü was born in Berlin; her Kurdish parents sent her back to their home village, Erzurum, Turkey, when she was 16, to marry a cousin. She later left him, taking her son with her; she moved into an apartment and attended school. She was 23 and finishing her training to become an electrician when on 7 February 2005 she was shot to death at a bus stop in Berlin. The police arrested her brothers, suspecting an honour killing, since she had received and reported numerous death threats. In September Ayhan Sürücü, the youngest brother, confessed to the murder. Turkish women took to the streets of Berlin to protest her killing. Muslim leaders in Berlin emphasized that there was no basis for honour killings in the Koran, but they were also criticized for not making a clear condemnation of them.[62]

Honour killings, of course, are comparatively very rare. Endorsement and approval of them, however, is not as rare as it ought to be. It is chilling to note that children on a school playground just yards from where Sürücü was gunned down were heard praising the murder because the victim had 'lived like a German'.

'I heard a young Turkish lady said on a Turkish radio station "she deserved it because she took off her headscarf". This is incredible,' says Ozcan Mutlu, one of the few Turks sitting on the Berlin city council.[63]

A BBC poll in 2006 found that one in ten Asians said they would condone the murder of someone who disrespected their family's honour.[64] A YouGov poll of Muslim students published in July 2008 found that 32 per cent of the students polled said killing in the name of religion can be justified.[65] The exemplary effect here is very important. Honour killings are rare, but they occur and are reported frequently enough to serve as a warning. They are also the end point of an extended pattern of coercion and control that is based less in parental discipline or uxorial protectiveness than in a concern with family honour, which is taken to be located between the legs of the female members of the family. Honour killing is rare, but coerced marriage is unfortunately not rare at all, and the two are intimately linked. Girls and women know that other girls and women have been murdered for refusing or escaping forced marriages, and this knowledge makes it very difficult for them to refuse. In short, honour killing is the rare end point of a great deal of lower-level bullying. It is unpleasantly reminiscent of lynching in the Jim Crow Southern USA: it sends a very strong warning to anyone inclined to rebel.

It is often claimed that forced marriage is geographical rather than religious, South Asian rather than Muslim or Sikh or Hindu. But religion gives traditions a backbone, and a veneer of justification, that make it easier to defend traditions and protect them from criticism.

The law is the law

On 8 September 2003 the Jordanian parliament overwhelmingly rejected a proposed law imposing harsher punishments for men who kill female relatives in honour killings. It was the second time in three months that the Chamber of Deputies quashed the bill on such killings. 'Islamists and conservatives opposed to the new law said it would encourage vice and destroy social values,' the BBC reported. 'Jordanian MPs argue that more lenient punishments will violate religious traditions and damage the fabric of Jordan's conservative society.' King Abdullah had passed a temporary bill imposing harsher punishments in 2001, but parliament dissolved the bill in 2008.[66]

Next day, 9 September, three brothers murdered their two sisters in an honour killing in Amman. Officials told the media the three brothers, who had been arrested, had admitted that they carried out the killing for reasons of 'family honour'. The elder sister, aged 27, had left her family home two years earlier to marry a man without her family's consent; her 20-year-old sister had later run away to join her. Having been informed where the sisters were, the brothers went to their home with axes, and hacked them to death. The elder sister's 10-month-old baby and her husband escaped unharmed.[67]

In Yemen in May 2008 Arwa Abdu Muhammad Ali walked out of her husband's house and ran to a local hospital, where she complained that he had been beating and sexually abusing her for eight months. She is 9 years old. The month before, Nujood Ali, aged 10, went by herself to a courthouse to demand a divorce, generating a landmark legal case. The two girls' stories, taken together, have prompted a movement to end child marriage in Yemen. But despite growing outrage, reform is not easy. Islamic conservatives defend the practice, pointing to the Prophet Muhammad's marriage to a 9-year-old.

> 'Voices are rising in society against this phenomenon and its catastrophes,' said Shawki al-Qadhi, an imam and opposition member in Parliament who has tried unsuccessfully to muster support for a legal

ban on child marriage in Yemen in the past. 'But despite rejections of it by many people and some religious scholars, it continues.'[68]

In March 2000 Egypt passed a reform to the divorce law that allowed women to divorce more easily; other reform, however, was blocked.

Opposition from religious conservatives and men who saw their domination of family life threatened required some compromise. As the legislation progressed, a provision allowing Egyptian women to travel without a husband's or father's permission was eliminated as too daring.[69]

Attempts to moderate harsh laws relating to women in Saudi Arabia invariably meet with conservative opposition. Attempts to win the right to drive cars are just one example. The ban on driving applies to all women in Saudi Arabia, whatever their nationality. It was originally unofficial, but became law in 1990, after 47 women challenged the authorities by taking their families' cars out for a drive. The Saudi religious authorities were outraged and the women were jailed for one day, their passports were confiscated, and many lost their jobs.[70]

Human Rights Watch said in a 2002 report on Iran that 'Conservative clerics taunted critics of corporal punishment, and accused them of being opposed to Islamic rule – in some cases even calling for the shedding of the blood of such critics.'[71] In September 2008 Iran sentenced four women's rights activists to six months in prison for writing articles on feminist websites. Parvin Ardalan, Jelveh Javaheri, Maryam Hosseinkhah and Nahid Keshavarz are members of an initiative that seeks to change Iran's Sharia-based laws for women by collecting one million signatures.[72]

So God does hate women?

Well, what can one say. These religious authorities and conservative clerics worship a wretchedly cruel unjust vindictive executioner of a

God. They worship a God of 10-year-old boys, a God of playground bullies, a God of rapists, of gangs, of pimps.

They worship – despite rhetoric about justice and compassion and agapē – a God who sides with the strong against the weak, a God who cheers for privilege and punishes egalitarianism. They worship a God who is a male and who gangs up with other males against women. They worship a thug.

They worship a God who thinks little girls should be married to grown men. They worship a God who looks on in approval when a grown man rapes a child because he is 'married' to her. They worship a God who thinks a woman should receive 80 lashes with a whip because her hair wasn't completely covered. They worship a God who is *pleased* when three brothers hack their sisters to death with axes because one of them married without their father's permission.

One wonders how they can stand it. One wonders how they can bear to worship and love and pray to a God of this kind – so brutal, so unjust, so petty, so stupid.

Language is powerful, however, and so is self-deception. The magic of simply endlessly saying, and believing, that God is love or that compassion is central to religion, is perhaps all the explanation that is required.

2 Religious Apologetics, Islam and Caricature

At 8.00 a.m. on Monday 11 March 2002, the pupils of Intermediate Girls' School No. 31 in Mecca, Saudi Arabia, were settling down for their first lesson of the day when a short-circuit in a faulty cooker sparked a fire in the school's tearoom.[1] The blaze that resulted was not large, but it sent black smoke billowing through the over-crowded classrooms. Half an hour later, 14 young girls were dead, crushed to death in the panic that had swept through the school as pupils and teachers, choking and terrified, tried to flee the burning building. Abdullah Bahadik, the first witness on the scene, reported that the broken bodies of the dead girls were piled up on top of each other at the bottom of the school's main staircase.

Death by fire, or by the panic induced by fire, is not uncommon. In the week of writing this, for example, fires in Russia have killed 75 people (and more than 10,000 people a year die in fires in that country). However, a common mark of these kinds of tragedies is that individuals will move mountains in their efforts to rescue people. One thinks of the iconic photograph of firefighter Mike Kehoe as he ascended the stairs of the World Trade Center on 9/11 against the rush of people fleeing the doomed tower. Or perhaps of Gavin Battensby, whose heroism in trying to save a child from a house fire was witnessed by a neighbour:

> When I looked through the window I saw the flames at Sherree's house and saw her stood at the bathroom window, screaming and screaming. I saw Gavin and he looked in a bad way, he looked really burned and

charred. He ran back into the house shouting. We could hear him saying 'I
can't find the baby.'[2]

At Intermediate Girls' School No. 31 things played out rather
differently. In a macabre inversion of the usual pattern of human
valour which sees people rushing into a burning building to rescue
survivors, the girls at this school were sent back into the smoke and
flames after they had already managed to escape. The reason for this
was that the Saudi religious police, who had turned up outside the
school, considered the girls to be inappropriately dressed for an
escape – apparently they had neglected to put on their *abayas*
(enveloping black head-to-toe robes) before running for their lives.

Incredibly what occurred that morning seems to have been even
worse than these bare facts would suggest.[3] The English language
newspaper *Arab News* reported that members of the Commission for
Promoting Virtue and Preventing Vice (as the religious police are
called in Saudi) obstructed rescue efforts by refusing to allow people
into the building to help with the evacuation (including some who
were carrying buckets of water to douse the fire); attacked people
who did try to help; and beat those girls – some as young as 13 –
who managed to leave the building without wearing their *abayas*.

The normal response to this kind of thing, and to the horrors we
documented in the first chapter, is to express outrage, but then to
suggest that it is associated with 'extremism' or 'fanaticism', and has
little or nothing to do with religion proper. This was the tack taken by
many commentators in the aftermath of the school-fire.

Nourah Abdul Aziz Al-Kheriji in *Arab News*:

> Why did they insist that the girls not leave the school without abayas and
> head-coverings? Weren't they aware that the girls were running for their
> very lives? Weren't they aware that they were only girls and not mature
> women? And even if they had been mature women, on what basis should
> anyone deny them escape from certain death? Aren't these people aware
> that Muslims are allowed to disregard what is normally forbidden in
> extraordinary circumstances of life and death?[4]

Mona Eltahawy in *The Washington Post*:

> What kind of virtue is it to allow girls to die in a fire because of what they were not wearing? Whose Islam is it that allows these men to dilute the faith I and millions of others cherish for its teachings of compassion and justice to nothing more than a dress code and sexual segregation? I grew up learning God is merciful and that faith was based on choice ...[5]

Khaled Abou El Fadl in *Global Dialogue*:

> Perhaps the most extreme form of Wahhabi fanaticism took place recently, on 11 March 2002, when the mutawwa'in (religious police) prevented schoolgirls from exiting a burning school in Mecca, or from being rescued by their parents or firemen, because they were not 'properly covered'.[6]

This general view that religion is in its essence benign, that true religious belief is somehow incompatible with intolerance, cruelty and viciousness, is a significant cultural trope in the modern West. Thus, for example, in her BBC Today/Chatham House lecture, Cherie Booth argued that all religions recognize the 'essential dignity' of each individual:

> Indeed, I would go further and say the very concept of human rights has its roots in the world's great religions. Whatever their differences, they converge in their understanding of the irreducible worth of each human being. Buddhism, Christianity, Hinduism, Islam, Judaism and others, all share profound ideas on the dignity and special worth of each individual ...[7]

It follows then that if religion is implicated in the subordination of women, it is likely the consequence of 'cultural pressures' or sexist male clerics rather than doctrines or practices that might be considered foundational for any particular religion. Hence Booth claims – incorrectly – that

> it is not laid down in the Koran that women can be beaten by their husbands or that their evidence should be devalued as it is in some Islamic Courts – and it is important too for judges and political leaders to

remind everyone that the philosophical purpose of Sharia is to protect and promote all human welfare.[8]

This view that religion is at root beneficent is the one almost invariably espoused by Western political leaders, especially when confronted by atrocities and injustices perpetrated in its name. George W. Bush, for example, has claimed that people of faith are united in a commitment to love their families, to protect their children, and to construct a more peaceful world;[9] Kofi Annan has argued that although religious practices may vary, they reflect the universal values of mercy, tolerance and love;[10] and Tony Blair has claimed variously that religious bigotry is inconsistent with true religion, that the major religions share common values and sentiments, and that there is a need for people to teach true theology in order to defeat those people who pervert it.[11]

More particularly, Jean Chrétien insisted in the aftermath of the events of 9/11 that the West had 'no quarrel with Islam', but rather with those terrorists whose acts of mass murder 'unjustly smeared a great world religion';[12] and the British Home Secretary, Jacqui Smith, echoed this sentiment in January 2008 when she used her first major speech to claim that Islamic terrorism is better understood as 'anti-Islamic activity', since there is 'nothing Islamic about the wish to terrorize, nothing Islamic about plotting murder, pain and grief'.[13]

Perhaps the most obvious point to make about this idea that religion is a force for the good is that it lacks *prima facie* plausibility. Religious texts might contain 'profound ideas on the dignity and special worth of each individual', but they're also full of murder, mayhem and violence. This is well known, of course, but it is easy to forget that the Abrahamic God in particular is brutal and bloodthirsty. The philosopher Stephen Law suggests that he is more akin to a mafia boss than a loving creator:

> He singles out one particular people as 'his', and controls them largely by fear. He demands sacrifices. He leads them in tribal wars and shows no mercy – demanding that even women and children should be put to the

sword. He conducts bizarre loyalty tests (God instructed Abraham to sacrifice his only son), has temper tantrums and is vindictive, inflicting ridiculously cruel and over-the-top punishments that can extend even to a transgressor's distant family and beyond.[14]

Thus, one might consider, for example, that the Bible reports that God destroyed the cities Sodom and Gomorrah, and all of their inhabitants;[15] killed more than 50,000 Israelites for peering into the Ark of the Covenant;[16] arranged for a prophet to be torn apart by a lion for the sin of disobedience;[17] caused Jehoram of Judah to suffer an intestinal affliction that made his bowels drop out;[18] and promised that 'wrath and fury' would greet those who chose the path of unrighteousness.[19]

If religion is suspect in its words, then it is no less so in its deeds (as we saw all too clearly in the first chapter). Its catalogue of atrocities and moral missteps is well known, of course: the Crusades (which led Saint Bernard of Clairvaux to declare that 'the Christian glories in the death of a pagan, because thereby Christ himself is glorified'); pogroms directed against the Jews; Islamic wars of conquest; Buddhist support for Japanese militarism; the barbarities of the Inquisition; the iniquities of the Hindu caste system; the brutal execution of apostates, heretics and infidels of all stripes; and so on, ad bloody infinitum.

The fact that religion has this dark aspect is not enough, of course, to persuade its apologists of its malign nature. A number of fairly standard arguments tend to be marshalled in its defence:

- If terrible things are done in the name of religion, it is because people have the habit of misunderstanding the *true* nature of religion, which is about mercy, tolerance and love.
- If religion is associated with some rather unfortunate practices, it is because of the warping effect of social, political and cultural factors.
- If atrocities are perpetrated in the name of religion, then they are no worse than those perpetrated in the name of no religion.

- If religion has its faults, then these are more than compensated for by the contribution that it makes to much that is good in the world.
- Religions are not static entities. Therefore the undesirable aspects of any particular religion are susceptible to reform and change.
- Religious belief isn't going away any time soon. The important thing is to work out how to live with it.

The significant point here is that it is precisely these sorts of arguments that are employed by people who wish to defend religion against the charge that it is misogynist. Islam poses a particular problem in this respect. As we saw in the previous chapter, the majority of the more egregious examples of religious misogyny seem to be associated with the religion of the Prophet. The relative lack of women's rights and sexual equality in large parts of the Muslim world is often taken to be a defining mark of a fundamental schism between Western liberalism and an Islamic authoritarianism rooted in the unquestioning acceptance of religious tradition. This puts the question of the treatment of women in the Koran, ahadith and sira on centre stage. Particularly, if one wants to argue that there is no fundamental incompatibility between Muslim and secular liberal values, and that true Islam is thoroughly egalitarian, then at the very least it is necessary to show that this is borne out by its texts and traditions. Or, to put this another way, if one wants to show that religious misogyny is a function of the distortions of culture and politics, then it is necessary to demonstrate that misogyny is a distortion in the first place.

The work of Karen Armstrong, one-time Roman Catholic nun, now an ecumenical warrior and bestselling author, is instructive in this respect. She argues that Islam properly understood is a religion of tolerance and peace; and, moreover, that the egalitarianism of Muhammad's original message included a commitment to the emancipation of women. In Armstrong's view, Western suspicion of Islam is rooted in prejudice and a distorted view of the religion followed by nearly a quarter of the world's population. It is necessary, therefore, for people in the West to

> learn to understand the Muslims with whom they share the planet. They must learn to respect and appreciate their faith, their needs, their anger, and their aspirations. And there can be no better place to start this essential process than with a more accurate knowledge of the life of the Prophet Muhammad, whose special genius and wisdom can illuminate these dark and frightening times.[20]

For people worried that Islam and women don't mix, Armstrong provides the happy reassurance that Muhammad 'was one of those rare men who truly enjoy the company of women';[21] and also that he was a proto-feminist:

> The emancipation of women was a project dear to the Prophet's heart. The Quran gave women rights of inheritance and divorce centuries before Western women were accorded such status. The Quran prescribes some degree of segregation and veiling for the Prophet's wives, but there is nothing in the Quran that requires the veiling of *all* women or their seclusion in a separate part of the house.[22]

The trouble with this line of argument is that there are aspects of Muhammad's life that are not entirely compatible with the idea that he had the best interests of women at heart. In particular, an issue that looms large is the age of Aisha – his favourite wife – at the time of their marriage. Indeed, it briefly became headline news in June 2002, when the Reverend Jerry Vines, then pastor of First Baptist Church in Jacksonville, Florida, and previously a president of the Southern Baptist Convention, publicly condemned the Prophet Muhammad as a 'demon-possessed paedophile' who had taken a 9-year-old girl to be his bride.

It is worth exploring the issue of Muhammad's marriage to Aisha, and Armstrong's treatment of it, in some detail. By doing so, we will get a sense of the strategies and techniques that apologists for religion employ to defend the idea that religion is a force for the good. It will also allow us to look at how women are treated in

the canonical texts and traditions of Islam, and to consider some of
the more specific theological, sociological and political issues
raised by the way that the Prophet is supposed to have treated
women.

Perhaps the key point here is that Muhammad's life is considered
exemplary for Muslims – it is the kind of life to which all Muslim men
should aspire – therefore, if it turns out that there are good reasons
for supposing that Muhammad did marry Aisha when she was still a
young child, there are large implications for how we should view
Islam's treatment of women. As Kecia Ali puts it in her timely and
brave analysis of this issue:

> If one accepts the hadith account of his marriage to Aishah, one confronts
> the actions of the Prophet in doing something that is unseemly, if not
> unthinkable, for Muslims in the West. Suggesting that he was wrong to do
> so raises profound theological quandaries. Yet accepting the rightness of
> his act raises the question: on what basis can one reject the marriage of
> young girls today? At stake are broader issues regarding the relevance of
> the prophetic example to Islamic sexual ethics and the relevance of
> historical circumstances to the application of precedent.[23]

Karen Armstrong for her part is not entirely clear about the issue of
Aisha's age at the time of her marriage to Muhammad. In her book
Islam: A Short History, she simply ignores the question, though she
insists that it is a mistake to think the Prophet spent his time basking
in sensual delight, and we are told that his wives were sometimes
more of a hindrance than a pleasure.

> As he formed his new super-tribe, he was anxious to forge marriage ties
> with some of his closest companions, to bind them firmly together. His
> favourite new wife was Aisha, the daughter of Abu Bakr ... Many of his
> other wives were older women, who were without protectors or were
> related to the chiefs of those tribes who became allies of the *ummah*.
> None of them bore the Prophet any children.[24]

In her two biographies of Muhammad, Armstrong is required to
confront the marriage issue more directly. Her technique in the first,

Muhammad: A Biography of the Prophet, is to turn the event into the literary equivalent of an *OK* magazine photo shoot.

> Finally about a month after she had arrived in Mecca, it was decided that it was time for the wedding of Muhammad with Aisha. She was still only nine years old, so there was no wedding feast and the ceremonial was kept to a minimum ... Abu Bakr had bought some fine red-striped cloth from Bahrein and this had been made into a wedding dress for her. Then they took her to her little apartment beside the mosque. There Muhammad was waiting for her, and he laughed and smiled while they decked her with jewellery and ornaments and combed her long hair. Eventually a bowl of milk was brought in and Muhammad and Aisha both drank from it. The marriage made little difference to Aisha's life. Tabari says that she was so young that she stayed at her parents' home and the marriage was consummated there later when she had reached puberty. Aisha went on playing with her girlfriends and her dolls.[25]

Armstrong does a good job here in making these events seem acceptable to a modern sensibility. She portrays Muhammad as a kind of indulgent uncle figure, rather than as a man in his early fifties about to take a prepubescent girl as his wife. However, even accepting the terms of Armstrong's account, there are aspects here that we should find disturbing. For example: 1) Aisha's marriage was something that *happened to her* at the behest of the powerful men in her life; 2) she was much too young to have offered anything like her informed consent, even if it had been sought; 3) neither puberty nor marriage entails that a sexual relationship is morally justified; and 4) the marriage was a kind of horse-trading – Aisha's hand for a familial tie to Abu Bakr.

It will be objected here that it is absurd to judge these events in terms of the standards of twenty-first-century morality. Thus, for example, in his book *No God but God*, Reza Aslan insists that Muhammad's actions need no defence:

> Like the great Jewish patriarchs Abraham and Jacob; like the prophets Moses and Hosea ... all Shaykhs in Arabia – Muhammad included – had

either multiple wives, multiple concubines, or both. And while
Muhammad's union with a nine-year-old girl may be shocking to our
modern sensibilities, his betrothal to Aisha was just that: *a betrothal*. Aisha
did not consummate her marriage to Muhammad until after reaching
puberty, which is when every girl in Arabia without exception became
eligible for marriage.[26]

However, this argument is not quite the Get Out Of Jail Free card that
it might be supposed. In particular, it is necessary to deal with two
rather thorny issues before presenting it to the jailer in the
expectation that the prison gates will swing open. First, it is at least
arguable that morality is not culturally or historically relative in the
way that this argument seems to suggest. This is a complex matter,
especially where it concerns issues of culpability, but consider, for
example, that it is quite possible to think that the practice of colonial
slavery was immoral, even if one accepts that by the standards
prevailing at the time it was not seen to be: in other words, it is quite
possible to think that slavery is wrong now and that it was wrong
then. Similarly, it is entirely possible to think that child marriage is
immoral, and has always been immoral, even if one accepts that it
hasn't always been seen to be immoral.

The second issue has to do with the relevance of Prophetic
example to present-day ethics. As we noted earlier, Muhammad's life
is considered exemplary within Islam; therefore, we're going to run
into difficulties if we want to cherry-pick which parts of his life and
behaviour we consider to be of relevance for ethics today. In other
words, there are difficulties in dismissing any of Muhammad's actions
as simply being the product of his time given the status accorded to
his life among Muslims. This is not to argue that there is no way out
of this dilemma, but it is nevertheless a dilemma.

It is clear then that even accepting Armstrong's description of
these events – or indeed Aslan's non-apologia – there are ethical
problems with Muhammad's marriage to Aisha. Moreover, there is
the further worry that perhaps Armstrong's account is not reliable on
this issue. Certainly, it all seems rather too good to be true: yes,

Muhammad married a 9-year-old, but don't worry everybody, he didn't consummate the marriage until she was much older. Phew!

The feeling that things are too good to be true is a frequent experience when reading Armstrong's writing on Islam. Consider, for example, her claim, noted above, that the emancipation of women was a project dear to the Prophet's heart.[27] To substantiate this view, she pursues two broad strategies, which rather pull against one another.

The first is to talk up the progressiveness of the Koran. In particular, she praises its provisions for divorce and inheritance;[28] the fact that it incorporates women within a quasi-legal framework of rights and responsibilities;[29] and its insistence upon the equality of men and women before God.

> We must remember what life had been like for women in the pre-Islamic period when female infanticide was the norm and when women had no rights at all. Like slaves, women were treated as an inferior species, who had no legal existence. In such a primitive world, what Muhammad achieved for women was extraordinary. The very idea that a woman could be a witness or could inherit anything at all in her own right was extraordinary.[30]

Her second strategy is to employ a defensive apologetics in order to explain away the more reactionary elements of the Koran's treatment of women. Polygamy, in particular, poses a challenge. Armstrong explains that this was 'not designed to improve the sex life of the boys', but rather it was a social arrangement instituted during a time of war that was designed to ensure that women were not left without protectors.[31] She also points out that while the Koran permits a man to take up to four wives, it stipulates that if he cannot be scrupulously fair to all his wives, he must remain monogamous.[32] In other words, polygamy is only allowed if it involves strict equality within a harem. (It is somewhat disconcerting then that she continually refers to Aisha as Muhammad's favourite wife.)[33]

Armstrong engages in similar apologetics when she deals with the issue of concubinage. We quoted her earlier as stating that many of Muhammad's wives were older women, and that none of them – aside from Khadija, his first wife – bore him any children. This is misleading: what Armstrong neglected to mention is that Muhammad had a further child with a concubine – an Egyptian slave girl, and Coptic Christian, called Mariyah.

The story of Muhammad's relationship with Mariyah does nothing to establish his credentials as a proto-feminist blazing a path towards female emancipation. Peter Lings describes its beginnings as follows:

> the ruler of Egypt sent a rich present of a thousand measures of gold, twenty robes of fine cloth, a mule, a she-ass and, as the crown of the gift, two Coptic Christian slave girls escorted by an elderly eunuch. The girls were sisters, Mariyah and Sirin, and both were beautiful, but Mariyah was exceptionally so, and the Prophet marvelled at her beauty. He gave Sirin to Hassan ibn Thabit, and lodged Mariyah in the nearby house where Safiyyah had lived before her apartment adjoining the Mosque was built. There he would visit her both by day and night …[34]

In other words, Muhammad was given two sisters, both slaves, as a gift – along with assorted animals, gold, some robes and a eunuch – he took the more beautiful sister as a lover, and gave away her less attractive sibling to an associate. It is very hard to spin this as the behaviour of a man with the project of female emancipation close to his heart, but Armstrong does her best:

> The Muqawqis of Egypt is said to have sent Muhammad a beautiful curly-haired Egyptian slave girl, a Coptic Christian called Maryam, and Muhammad took her as his concubine. He used to visit her daily, spending more and more time with her, probably finding it a relief to escape the jealous atmosphere of the harem. Nobody would have found this odd. The Torah had made provision for concubinage, when the Israelites were at a similar stage of changing from the nomadic to the settled life.[35]

Unfortunately for Armstrong, whether or not Muhammad's contemporaries would have found this odd is not the point here. Rather, what is at stake is the morality of his behaviour. Kecia Ali expresses this point clearly:

> it is almost unimaginable today by many Muslims that a sexual relationship between a man and a female slave bound to him only by the tie of ownership and not matrimony could be legal, much less moral. And yet, since the Prophet is the standard for morality, the exemplar of uprightness, the question of his actions – both personal and as a leader of Muslims – takes on importance.[36]

However, although Armstrong's apologia misses the point – which actually says something rather worrying about her moral compass – it is worth spending a little time looking at its structure, since it is indicative of her general approach.

The first point to make is that her arguments and assertions are not properly referenced. This allows her to psychologize about motive, emotion, state of mind, and so on, without having to justify claims that seem to be based on little more than guesswork fuelled by wishful thinking.[37] For example, she begins the section on Mariyah by suggesting that her arrival on the scene was the highpoint of Muhammad's year and a source of 'great personal joy'.[38] She also suggests, as we have seen, that the reason he enjoyed visiting her was to escape the 'jealous atmosphere of the harem'. The combined effect here is to dignify Muhammad's relationship with Mariyah: he was not simply using his status and power in order to gain sexual access to a beautiful young woman, but was seeking joy and solace in her company. Presumably Armstrong's intention – whether conscious or otherwise – is to attenuate the moral worry that Mariyah was a mere instrument for the satisfaction of Muhammad's desires, bound to him by ownership, but not by fellow feeling.

The problem is that even if one accepts this sanitized version of events, Muhammad does not behave well by modern lights. As much as Armstrong would like to suggest that he was just visiting Mariyah for tea and cakes, she cannot eradicate the sexual aspect completely (not least because Mariyah quickly became pregnant by Muhammad). Therefore, she runs into the brute fact that Muhammad, an ageing tribal patriarch, was having a sexual relationship with a much younger woman, over whom he had ownership rights, and who was utterly dependent upon him for her well-being. In this situation, there is no such thing as consent, which means that by the standards of the present day Muhammad was behaving badly.[39] It is necessary then for Armstrong to add an extra element to her apologia: she tells us that this was all quite normal back then, and that the Jews also went in for concubinage. This is the tactic we met earlier of relativizing morality by suggesting that it is only appropriate to judge behaviour in terms of the moral standards prevailing when it occurred. The trouble is, as we have already noted, this argument doesn't work so well when applied to a person such as Muhammad who is considered exemplary. Here, no doubt inadvertently, Armstrong explains why:[40]

> ... Muslims seek to imitate Muhammad in their daily lives in order to approximate as closely as possible to this perfection and so to come as close as they can to God himself ... The *sunnah* taught Muslims to imitate the way Muhammad spoke, ate, loved, washed and worshipped so that in the smallest details of their lives they are reproducing his life on earth and in a real but symbolic sense bringing him to life once more.[41]

There is another interesting aspect of Armstrong's apologia that is worth commenting on; namely, that it is highly selective in terms of the content it features. For example, she neglects to mention about concubinage: that after the massacre of Qurayzah, Muhammad allowed the male victors to take their pick of the defeated tribe's women, and that he himself took a concubine – Rayhanah, a woman of great beauty, who remained his slave until she died;[42] that early Muslim scholars were generally agreed that the practice of using captured females for sexual gratification was sanctioned by the Koran;[43] that the ahadith report that Muhammad had the opportunity to repudiate this practice, but did not do so;[44] and that Prophetic example and religious precedent have been invoked in Muslim defences of slavery.[45]

Not surprisingly, Armstrong's sins of omission extend far beyond her treatment of the issue of concubinage. Particularly, as we have already seen, she tends to ignore or downplay evidence from the Koran, ahadith and sirah that suggests that Muhammad's religious tolerance and his commitment to female emancipation did not go very deep. A number of examples will suffice to make this clear.

First, Armstrong states that Islam makes men and women equal before God, but forgets to make it clear that this does not entail equality *tout court*. Consider, for example, that the Koran notoriously contains the following lines: 'If you fear high-handedness from your wives, remind them [of the teachings of God], then ignore them when you go to bed, then hit them.'[46] In *No God but God*, Reza Aslan deals with the misogynist implications of this passage by raising the (somewhat implausible) possibility that it has been mistranslated.[47] Armstrong, in contrast, has nothing to say at all about it.

Second, Armstrong is very quiet about Islam's treatment of the question of male sexual access to females. Muhammad is cited in the ahadith as denying that a wife has the right to refuse her husband's sexual advances.[48] This is echoed in the Koran, which contains the following verse: 'Women are your fields, so go into your fields when you please. Do good works and fear God.' Irshad Manji reports being shocked when she first read this verse:

> Huh? Go into women as you please, yet do good? Are women partners or property of men? Partners, insists Jamal Badawi, a renowned Quranic scholar ... Like fields, women need tender loving care in order to turn sperm into human beings. The farmer's 'seed is worthless unless you have the fertile land that will give it growth,' Badawi says, looking quite satisfied with his progressive explanation. But he has only addressed the words, 'Go into your fields.' What about the words, 'when you please'? Doesn't that quantifier give men undue power?[49]

It is not possible to know what Armstrong thinks about this because she does not discuss it. This is puzzling given her view that the emergence of Islam was good news for women.

Third, although Armstrong notes with approval that the Koran granted women certain rights of divorce, she is very sketchy on the detail. Particularly, she wisely omits to mention that the Koran allows a husband to divorce his wife irrevocably simply by repudiating her three times ('I divorce you, I divorce you, I divorce you'), a privilege which does not extend in the opposite direction.[50] Kecia Ali argues that Islamic legal doctrines about divorce derived from the Koran were fairly bleak for women, though she notes that in practice some flexibility was forthcoming. This is a reversal of Armstrong's usual line that history and circumstances have diluted the progressive nature of Muhammad's revelation.

There is evidence then that Armstrong is selective in what she reveals about Islam. The effect of this is to strip away the complexity that makes the Koran, and the life and words of Muhammad, morally suspect. She gives us a sugar-coated version of the religion that stretches credibility precisely because it strives so hard to fit in with modern values. This point brings us back to the question of Muhammad's marriage to Aisha. We noted earlier that Armstrong's version of events just seems too good to be true: the indulgent tribal patriarch marries 9-year old Aisha, but refrains from consummating the marriage until she reaches puberty. In her most recent biography of the Prophet, *Muhammad: A Prophet for Our Time*, she describes the marriage as follows:

> Abu Bakr was ... anxious to forge a closer link with the Prophet, and proposed that he should marry his daughter 'A'isha, who was then six years old. 'A'isha was formally betrothed to Muhammad in a ceremony at which the little girl was not present ... There was no impropriety in Muhammad's betrothal to 'A'isha. Marriages conducted in absentia to seal an alliance were often contracted at this time between adults and minors who were even younger than 'A'isha. This practice continued in Europe well into the early modern period. There was no question of

> consummating the marriage until 'A'isha reached puberty, when she
> would have been married off like any other girl.[51]

This passage is perfectly constructed to reassure modern readers that
there was nothing unseemly about these events. Its subtext is clear:
sex was not on the Prophet's mind when he married Aisha. Thus, we
learn variously: 1) that the marriage was not Muhammad's idea; 2)
that the betrothal made no difference to Aisha's life – she wasn't even
at the ceremony; 3) that it was normal at this time for marriages to be
conducted in absentia between adults and minors; 4) that this was
not a peculiarly Islamic practice; and 5) that there is no doubt that
Muhammad waited until Aisha reached puberty before consummating the marriage.

We have already seen that this kind of apologia, even on its own
terms, is not a moral escape hatch: the fact that Muhammad's actions
were culturally appropriate is not enough to establish their rectitude.
However, given Armstrong's penchant for selective reporting, there is
now the added worry that perhaps we are not being told the whole
truth here. Part of what arouses suspicion is that she does not
properly reference the account(s) she gives of Muhammad's marriage
to Aisha, which means that we don't know what evidence, if any,
justifies her version of events. It also makes it quite difficult to check
the detail of her account(s) against the historical record, especially
when one considers that the canonical histories of early Islam – those
of Ibn Ishaq, Ibn Sa'd, Tabari and Waqidi – were constructed out of an
oral tradition that was internally inconsistent.

There is, however, one instance where Armstrong departs from
her self-imposed moratorium on evidence, and it is precisely in
support of her claim that Muhammad waited until Aisha reached
puberty before having sex with her.

> She was still only nine years old, so there was no wedding feast and the
> ceremonial was kept to a minimum ... Tabari says that she [Aisha] was so
> young that she stayed at her parents' home and the marriage was
> consummated there later when she had reached puberty.[52]

In fact, Tabari – generally considered the best historian of early Islam – provides a number of different accounts of Muhammad's marriage to Aisha, almost all of which directly contradict this claim. For example, he cites Aisha herself as follows:

> The Messenger of God came to our house and the men and women of the *Ansâr* gathered around him ... I was then brought [in] while the Messenger of God was sitting on a bed in our house. [My mother] made me sit on his lap and said, 'These are your relatives. May God bless you with them and bless them with you!' Then the men and women got up and left. The Messenger of God consummated his marriage with me in my house when I was nine years old.[53]

This passage is immediately followed by two further accounts, which relate the same basic story. It is sufficient to quote just one of them:

> The Messenger of God saw 'A'ishah twice – [first when] it was said to him that she was his wife (she was six years old at that time), and later [when] he consummated his marriage with her after coming to Medina when she was nine years old.[54]

It is this version of events, rather than Armstrong's *Mills and Boon* version, that is the standard in the ahadith and sirah. It appears in the *Two Sahihs* – the hadith collections of Bukhari and Muslim, which Sunni Muslims consider to be the most authentic; and also in the histories of Ibn Ishaq, Ibn Sa'd and, later, Ibn Kathir. Moreover, as Kecia Ali reports, none of the classical sources specifically link Aisha's menarche with the consummation of her marriage.[55] Armstrong's claim that Tabari says that the Prophet's marriage to Aisha was consummated at puberty is not borne out by even a cursory examination of his text. Almost all of the traditions that he cites put Aisha's age at 9 (or 10) at consummation, and they make no mention of puberty.

It should be noted, however, that potentially there is some wriggle room here for Armstrong. Tabari's history, and indeed the ahadith, comprises a series of mainly oral accounts that are linked by chains of transmission – *isnad* – back to their original sources. Inevitably, there are inconsistencies in these accounts, and more general doubts about their reliability. This has allowed defenders of the view that Aisha had reached puberty before her marriage was consummated to question the veracity of those traditions that suggest otherwise; and also to construct alternative narratives about Aisha's age that depend on her being a 'girl' when some specific event occurred.

However, this line of defence is not easily open to Armstrong. Partly this is because she talks up the reliability of those canonical texts that put Aisha's age at 9 years old at consummation. But, more importantly, it is because she makes a *definitive* and *unqualified* claim about Aisha's age: she states that there was *no question* of consummating the marriage until Aisha reached puberty. This is untrue and indefensible. Not only is there a question about it, but it is an issue that has been debated, and is still being debated, in works of both criticism and apologetics. Moreover, it is by no means only Western critics of Islam who argue that textual evidence supports the proposition that Aisha was 9 years old at consummation. It is also the position of modern-day Muslim scholars such as Syed Suleman Nadvi, Muhammad Ali Al-Hanooti and Abdurrahman Robert Squires.

There is something quite shocking about Armstrong's unreliability on this issue. It seems inconceivable that she does not know that the balance of textual evidence supports the view that Aisha was 9 years old when her marriage was consummated (even if this issue hasn't been settled definitively), yet in her two biographies of Muhammad she implies that it is an established fact that consummation occurred at puberty. Unfortunately, she is not alone among the new wave of popularizers of Islam in adopting such a cavalier attitude towards the truth. Reza Aslan, for example, makes exactly the same claim about Aisha's age in his book *No God but God* (and also manages to get mixed up between Aisha's betrothal and her marriage, which cynics will not be surprised to learn turns out to be very convenient for the purpose of defending Muhammad's reputation on this issue).[56]

A possible response here might be to claim that while the issue of Muhammad's marriage to Aisha is of historical and theological interest, it has little significance for understanding Islam in the present day; and therefore the fact that Armstrong does not tell the whole truth about this issue is not terribly important, and indeed might be justified to the extent that it lessens the risk of inflaming the already tense relations between Muslims and non-Muslims in the West. There is something to this argument: for example, it is certainly true that Aisha's age has been used as a weapon by far right political groups to bash Muslims (where religion in effect functions as a proxy for race). However, where the argument falls down is that Muhammad's marriage to Aisha is actually more important for understanding modern Islam than it might at first be supposed.

Consider, for example, that the practice of child marriage is widespread in the Islamic world. A recent UNICEF report showed that 54 per cent of girls in Afghanistan are married by the age of 18; 44 per cent of women aged between 20 and 24 in Niger had married when they were under the age of 15; in Egypt, 44 per cent of rural women who married in the mid-1980s were under the age of 16 at the time; and 5 per cent of Bangladeshi girls between the ages of 10 and 14 are married.[57] Although it would be a massive over-simplification to claim that Islam is the cause of these patterns, it is nevertheless the case that Islamic beliefs are sometimes a factor in child marriage.

The case of the Yemen is instructive here. In 1998, the Yemeni parliament revised a 1992 law that had set the minimum age of marriage at 15. The new ruling allowed girls to be married much earlier, so long as they did not move in with their husbands until they had reached sexual maturity. This has been interpreted by conservative clerics to mean that the consummation of a marriage can take place at the age of 9. *The New York Times* reports that 'the change reflected the triumph of northern Yemen's more conservative Islamic culture over the secular and Marxist south.'[58] Human rights activists have fought to reverse this ruling, but to date they have been unsuccessful, thwarted by Islamic clerics who precisely point to Muhammad's marriage to Aisha in order to justify their views. A similar struggle has been played out in Iran. After the 1979 revolution, the minimum age of marriage was reduced to 9 years old for girls. In the year 2000, under pressure from women's rights activists, the Iranian parliament voted to raise the minimum age to 15. However, this change was vetoed by the Council of Guardians, a legislative oversight body dominated by traditional Islamic clerics, which claimed that the new ruling was contrary to Islamic law. (It is also interesting to note here that the Ayatollah Khomeini himself married a 10-year-old girl when he was 28.)

This brings us back to an issue that we raised towards the beginning of this chapter: the fact that the absence of women's rights and sexual equality in large parts of the Muslim world is often taken to be a defining mark of a fundamental schism between Western liberalism and Islamic authoritarianism. Karen Armstrong's *modus operandi* is to minimize the grounds of such a schism by arguing that Islam properly understood is egalitarian and tolerant. However, the reality is that it is no such thing: not because it is inegalitarian and intolerant – though, as we have seen, it certainly has these aspects, especially with respect to the treatment of women – but because it has always been a complex, multifaceted and contradictory social formation, whose character cannot possibly be captured in the terms of such an absurdly simple formula.

Armstrong's writings on Islam are an exercise in caricature. Her desire to sanitize and Westernize Islam means that she produces an account of the religion that is tendentious, incomplete and patronizing.

3   The World and the Kitchen

Human beings have to live together. We can live together at a distance or close up, but we have to live in social groups of one kind or another; life on a desert island is too nasty, brutish and short to bear. Living off the grid is too much work; we depend on our infrastructures; we do much better by pooling our resources.

Needing to live together, then, we need to manage each other. Animals manage each other with hierarchies, threats, displays, aggression, submission, alliances, bribes, rewards, punishments and exchanges. Humans do much the same, but elaborated language and writing enable us to do it with exponentially greater detail and explicitness. Holy Books are very useful for this.

Management is just management; it's not justice or morality or fairness. The top dog or stag or chimp isn't necessarily the best in some general (much less ethical) sense, it's just the biggest and strongest. Human arrangements for interpersonal management have historically tended to follow this pattern.

This is especially true when it comes to the explicit detailed language-based management codes that are exclusive to humans. Whatever arrangements people make in private, the official rules have been strikingly unabashed about favouring the stronger party. Men are stronger therefore they should have all the power, we were told explicitly or implicitly for millennia, as John Stuart Mill pointed out.

Laws and systems of polity always begin by recognizing the relations they find already existing between individuals. They convert what was a mere physical fact into a legal right, give it the sanction of society, and principally aim at the substitution of public and organised means of asserting and protecting these rights, instead of the irregular and lawless conflict of physical strength ... If people are mostly so little aware how completely, during the greater part of the duration of our species, the law of force was the avowed rule of general conduct, any other being only a special and exceptional consequence of peculiar ties – and from how very recent a date it is that the affairs of society in general have been even pretended to be regulated according to any moral law; as little do people remember or consider, how institutions and customs which never had any ground but the law of force, last on into ages and states of general opinion which never would have permitted their first establishment.[59]

But there is a great deal of elaboration between a bite or bark or show of canine teeth, and the niqab and the Virgin Mary and female genital mutilation, and all of it is subject to interpretation.

Division of labour is a branch of management. If it is systematized and made socially mandatory, via tradition, law or religious edict, that saves everyone the trouble of figuring out who does what over and over again, one at a time, generation after generation. It also spares everyone the difficulty and stress of disagreement, arguing, fighting, and the nuisance of bargaining, compromise, adjustment. The management is done in advance, from the top down, so that it is placed (ideally) beyond dispute.

This probably seems especially desirable between men and women because they are so intimately entangled with one another. Quarrels between races or classes can be kept at a distance at least some of the time, but family disputes are up close and personal. This may be why many people (mostly men) are still willing to attempt to manage and subordinate women when they wouldn't attempt the same with any other group.

The trouble is, the management does all that at a very high price. It renders more than half of all human beings permanently subordinate to the other fraction, and it removes their ability to choose a plan of life for themselves. It also gives men power over women and it is well known of power that it is subject to abuse. Finally it teaches women that they are officially inferior, from birth, no matter what qualities or talents they may turn out to have.

It's a high price to pay, but since the price was paid by the subordinated, those doing the subordinating considered it well worth the cost, and in much of the world they still do.

History has moved on, however; things have changed since Pericles told the women of Athens that their glory was in not being spoken of. Urbanization, industrialization, printing, mass education, mass media, globalization, the UN, NGOs have all changed the equation and still do. Even isolated villages aren't guaranteed to be immune. There may be a radio, or a TV, or a visiting reporter, or someone from a local or international NGO. There are influences and ideas hinting that it's not written in stone that men are born to command and women to obey. In short there's always a danger now that any woman anywhere can become aware that not all women are subordinate or secluded or incompetent. This means that people who want to keep women subordinate have to cast about for help with that project; one of the most useful places to look is religion.

Because religion is useful for this it is in many ways a special case. Religion has a lot of special dispensations and immunities and benefits of the doubt that enable it to say things that pretty much any other human institution would now shrink from. The pronouncements it makes about women are conspicuous examples. The more conservative religions and clerics offer generalizations about women that would be laughed off the stage if offered by a judge or an academic or a politician.

The approach the clerics take, with a remarkable degree of ecumenical trans-credal agreement, is to say, over and over again, that women and men are equal but different, that they are 'complementary'. This complementary difference means they have different (but complementary) roles in life, which (by a striking coincidence) turn out to be the roles they've always had – men for the world, women for home and family.

This is the law of the creator

Myra Bradwell passed the Illinois bar exam in 1869 but was denied admission to the Illinois Bar; she filed suit, claiming that refusing to admit her to the bar because she was female violated her Fourteenth Amendment rights. Her case reached the Illinois Supreme Court, which ruled that the Privileges or Immunities Clause of the Fourteenth Amendment did not include the right to practise a profession. She took her case to the US Supreme Court, which ruled against her in 1872. Justice Bradley concurred in the decision:

> the civil law, as well as nature herself, has always recognized a wide difference in the respective spheres and destinies of man and woman. Man is, or should be, woman's protector and defender. The natural and proper timidity and delicacy which belongs to the female sex evidently unfits it for many of the occupations of civil life. The constitution of the family organization, which is founded in the divine ordinance, as well as in the nature of things, indicates the domestic sphere as that which properly belongs to the domain and functions of womanhood. The harmony, not to say identity, of interest and views which belong, or should belong, to the family institution is repugnant to the idea of a woman adopting a distinct and independent career from that of her husband ... The paramount destiny and mission of woman are to fulfil the noble and benign offices of wife and mother. This is the law of the Creator.[60]

Well, that was 1872. The world has changed out of all recognition since then. No one says things like that anymore, surely, at least not in the developed world.

In the USA a group of pastors and scholars established The Council on Biblical Manhood and Womanhood in 1987 to 'address their concerns over the influence of feminism not only in our culture but also in evangelical churches'.

> In opposition to the growing movement of feminist egalitarianism they articulated what is now known as the complementarian position which affirms that men and women are equal in the image of God, but maintain complementary differences in role and function. In the home, men lovingly are to lead their wives and family as women intelligently are to submit to the leadership of their husbands. In the church, while men and women share equally in the blessings of salvation, some governing and teaching roles are restricted to men.[61]

This is a blunt statement of male superiority and female subordination, but it is also carefully worded. On the one hand it offers an approach that is explicitly not egalitarian (except 'in the image of God' where it doesn't really make anything happen), but on the other hand it gives a flattering picture of the arrangement. Men are to lead their wives lovingly and women are to submit intelligently: that neatly reverses the expected pattern, and with it the logic. One would expect 'lead intelligently' and 'submit lovingly' – but it appears that even The Council on Biblical Manhood and Womanhood doesn't want to say, quite so overtly, that men are to lead their wives because men are intelligent and women are to submit because women are loving. The Council doesn't want to *come right out and say* that men are to lead their wives because women are stupid. The Council, in short, wants to sugar the pill.

The problem there of course is that if women intelligently submit it is not clear why they submit at all. It is not clear why wives and husbands can't simply be equal, with no one submitting to anyone. People in the wider world manage that: women and men work together as colleagues and in hierarchies with some women higher than some men. The latter arrangement still upsets the sense of fitness of some, but on the whole it seems normal and inevitable, while any moves to prevent it now would seem 1) grossly unfair; and 2) cripplingly inefficient. The Council on Biblical Manhood & Womanhood's flattering wording leaves its reasoning conspicuously naked.

The Council has something it calls 'The Danvers Statement on

Biblical Manhood and Womanhood', which includes among its 'Affirmations' the following:

Distinctions in masculine and feminine roles are ordained by God as part of the created order, and should find an echo in every human heart (Gen 2:18, 21–24; 1 Cor 11:7–9; 1 Tim 2:12–14).

Adam's headship in marriage was established by God before the Fall, and was not a result of sin (Gen 2:16–18, 21–24, 3:1–13; 1 Cor 11:7–9).

Both Old and New Testaments also affirm the principle of male headship in the family and in the covenant community (Gen 2:18; Eph 5:21–33; Col 3:18–19; 1 Tim 2:11–15).

In the family, husbands should forsake harsh or selfish leadership and grow in love and care for their wives; wives should forsake resistance to their husbands' authority and grow in willing, joyful submission to their husbands' leadership (Eph 5:21–33; Col 3:18–19; Tit 2:3–5; 1 Pet 3:1–7).

In the church, redemption in Christ gives men and women an equal share in the blessings of salvation; nevertheless, some governing and teaching roles within the church are restricted to men (Gal 3:28; 1 Cor 11:2–16; 1 Tim 2:11–15).[62]

In a similar vein, the evangelical Patrick Henry College in Purcelville, Virginia, declares that its mission is to

prepare Christian men and women who will lead our nation and shape our culture with timeless biblical values and fidelity to the spirit of the American founding.

Patrick Henry has a 'Statement of Faith' to which it requires each 'trustee, officer, faculty member, and student of the College, as well as all other employees and agents of the College as may be specified by resolution of the Board of Trustees, shall fully and enthusiastically subscribe',[63] along with a 'Statement of Biblical Worldview' which is 'attested to by all trustees, administrators, and faculty' and which includes some rules about marriage and women and men:

The Lord is the author of the union of marriage, made evident when He provided a companion for the first man, Adam. This design resembles the unique relationship of Christ and His bride, the church. Therefore, marriage is a sacred God-made union between a man and a woman, which is to be separated by no man. It is to model the reverence, love, sacrifice, and respect exemplified by Christ for His bride. Husbands are the head of their wives just as Christ is the head of the church, and are to love their wives just as Christ loved the church and gave Himself up for her.[64]

A wife is to submit herself graciously

In June 1998 the Southern Baptist Convention amended its 'Faith and Message Statement' to include a declaration that 'a wife is to submit herself graciously to the servant leadership of her husband'.[65] This was only the second time the Statement had been amended; the previous amendment was in 1963 when a section on higher education was added. The Statement is not a mandate, and no Baptist is required to agree with it, but it is a central theological proclamation, and Southern Baptist employees, seminary professors, and ministers are expected to agree with it. Some Baptists left the Convention because of the amendment; former US President Jimmy Carter was one of them and had this to say in a book on the rise of reactionary evangelicalism:

> Women are greatly abused in many countries in the world, and the alleviation of their plight is made less likely by the mandated subservience of women by Christian fundamentalists.[66]

Dorothy Patterson is married to Paige Patterson, President of the Southern Baptists, and was on the seven-member committee that amended the Statement; she wrote about her views in a *New York Times* article in 1998 in which she wrote an imagined reply to an 1857 letter by Susan B. Anthony.

> We must not abrogate the directives God has given for relationships between husbands and wives and for responsibilities of parents to their children. To do so opens the door for a society in which the marriages fail, children become violent and society itself abandons all absolutes ... From

my perspective, for a woman who chooses to marry, happiness and productivity will come from willingly submitting herself to the servant leadership of her husband, thereby coming under his provision and protection.[67]

Compared with chopped-off genitals and honour killings and young girls taken out of school to marry strangers, this bit of theological etiquette-mongering seems very mild, but it's interesting all the same. It's interesting because it seems like a very risky, indeed foolhardy policy, even in the Southern Baptists' own terms, and that fact raises questions about why they think it's worth the risk. Why is it so important to declare women officially subordinate? So important that it trumps obvious prudential considerations? It's hard to think of answers to that question that do not seem sinister in their implications.

The policy seems risky for the obvious reason that it either ignores or doesn't object to the possibility that a husband can ever be wrong. Saying that wives should graciously submit to their husbands seems to assume that the husbands will always have better judgement, will always want to do the right thing, will never make a decision that is selfish or short-sighted or ungenerous or dishonest. It seems highly unlikely that the Southern Baptist Convention could actually think this; it seems highly unlikely that their experience and observation of the world leads them to think that men are always right and women are always wrong in cases of disagreement. If that's accurate, it means the Southern Baptist Convention is willing to tell wives they should graciously submit to their husbands whether they are right or wrong – indeed that they *have* told them this, implicitly, because there is no stipulation or reservation in the amendment saying 'unless they are quite certain that their husbands are morally mistaken'. There is no conscience clause.

Why does the SBC not worry about the dangers of this? Why does it not worry about strayed sheep and prodigal sons? Why does it not worry about women – and children – at the mercy of men who drink too much, who spend all the money on themselves, who are violent, who commit crimes? Why does it give such bad advice?

Paige Patterson said the amendment was a response to 'a time of growing crisis in the family'.[68] But that explains nothing. Will families thrive if women become submissive and thus compromise their ability to discuss problems, disagree with decisions, attempt to reason with faulty judgement? It is hard to see why they would. In fact one can imagine an unintended consequence by which Southern Baptist women become much more cautious about marrying at all, because knowing they will be expected to submit graciously, they will want to be sure they marry a paragon of reason and virtue.

The SBC cites various biblical passages in its Statement, but in public it also offers reasons, so the reasons are there to be questioned, and the problems remain. What makes the SBC think it is always safe to assume that the husband's judgement is good enough to submit to? If they don't worry about the wife, why do they not worry about the children? Why do Southern Baptists in general not worry that many men will *use* such arbitrary authority to do whatever they like and still live in the odour of sanctity?

In March 1997 the First Baptist Church of Berryville Arkansas abruptly closed its day care center. The church told parents in a letter announcing the closing that working mothers 'neglect their children; damage their marriages and set a bad example', adding

> God intended for the home to be the center of a mother's world. In Titus 2:5, women are instructed to be 'discreet, chaste, keepers at home, good and obedient to their own husbands.'[69]

To be fair, this is not a universal view even among Baptists; another Berryville church promptly opened a day care center across town. Nevertheless, it is hard to imagine a secular institution making such a statement. Without Titus 2:5, what reason could it offer?

The Vatican takes the same view, in much the same words.

The Australian Catholic Bishops Conference Office for the

Participation of Women celebrated International Women's Day with a special Mass and lunch on 7 March 2008. Kimberly Davis, the Director of the Office for the Participation of Women, said there:

> The report on the participation of women in the Catholic Church in Australia published in 1999, *Woman and Man: One in Christ Jesus*, identified gender equality as the dominant issue. This called for the equal dignity of women and men created in the image and likeness of God to be recognised. This understanding of equality did not imply the sameness of men and women, but rather their complementarity and mutuality.[70]

In 1988 Pope John Paul II issued the encyclical *Mulieris Dignitatem* in which he issued women a lot of instructions.

> Even the rightful opposition of women to what is expressed in the biblical words 'He shall rule over you' (*Gen* 3:16) must not under any condition lead to the 'masculinization' of women. In the name of liberation from male 'domination', women must not appropriate to themselves male characteristics contrary to their own feminine 'originality'. There is a well-founded fear that if they take this path, women will not 'reach fulfilment', but instead will *deform and lose what constitutes their essential richness* ...[71]

Italics his. Women must not steal characteristics that belong to men but must stay as sweet as they are.

> The personal resources of femininity are certainly no less than the resources of masculinity: they are merely different. Hence a woman, as well as a man, must understand her 'fulfilment' as a person, her dignity and vocation, on the basis of these resources, according to the richness of the femininity which she received on the day of creation ...[72]

Women and men are different, and they 'must' act accordingly. To belabour the point, this is not equality.

In 1995 the Vatican issued a 'Letter to Women'.

> The creation of woman is thus marked from the outset by *the principle of help*: a help which is not one-sided but *mutual*. Woman complements man, just as man complements woman: men and women are

complementary. Womanhood expresses the 'human' as much as manhood does, but in a different and complementary way.

When the Book of Genesis speaks of 'help', it is not referring merely to *acting*, but also to *being.* Womanhood and manhood are complementary *not only from the physical and psychological points of view*, but also from the *ontological.* It is only through the duality of the 'masculine' and the 'feminine' that the 'human' finds full realization.

...

In this perspective of 'service' – which, when it is carried out with freedom, reciprocity and love, expresses the truly 'royal' nature of mankind – one can also appreciate that the presence of *a certain diversity of roles* is in no way prejudicial to women, provided that this diversity is not the result of an arbitrary imposition, but is rather an expression of what is specific to being male and female.[73]

In 2004 came the 'Letter to the Bishops of the Catholic Church on the Collaboration of Men and Women in the Church and in the World', which started off by saying that 'The Church, expert in humanity, has a perennial interest in whatever concerns men and women.' It is a nice question, what it is that makes the Catholic Church 'expert in humanity', given that its field is theology rather than anthropology, given that most of its staff are clerics rather than psychologists, and given that it excludes more than half of humanity from the priesthood and thus from all of the top positions. The Letter was written by Joseph Ratzinger and signed by John Paul II.[74]

In order to avoid the domination of one sex or the other, their differences tend to be denied, viewed as mere effects of historical and cultural conditioning. In this perspective, physical difference, termed *sex*, is minimized, while the purely cultural element, termed *gender,* is emphasized to the maximum and held to be primary. The obscuring of the difference or duality of the sexes has enormous consequences on a variety of levels ...

This perspective has many consequences. Above all it strengthens the idea that the liberation of women entails criticism of Sacred Scripture, which would be seen as handing on a patriarchal conception of God nourished by an essentially male-dominated culture ...

The ancient Genesis narrative allows us to understand how woman, in her deepest and original being, exists 'for the other' (cf. *1 Cor* 11:9) ...

From the first moment of their creation, man and woman are distinct, and will remain so for all eternity. Placed within Christ's Paschal mystery, they no longer see their difference as a source of discord to be overcome by denial or eradication, but rather as the possibility for collaboration, to be cultivated with mutual respect for their difference. From here, new perspectives open up for a deeper understanding of the dignity of women and their role in human society and in the Church.[75]

Rosemary Ganley commented in the *Catholic New Times* that 'All three letters have been unpersuasive, based on a fatal dual anthropology, which places the male as the norm of humanity, female as "other," always, it seems, the object study of what ails the human family.'[76]

The Pope's address at a convention on 'Woman and Man: The Humanum in its Entirety' in 2008 struck the same note.

This 'uni-duality' of man and woman is based on the foundation of the dignity of every person created in the image and likeness of God, who 'male and female he created them' (Gn 1: 27), avoiding an indistinct uniformity and a dull and impoverishing equality as much as an irreconcilable and conflictual difference ... Faced with cultural and political trends that seek to eliminate, or at least cloud and confuse, the sexual differences inscribed in human nature, considering them a cultural construct, it is necessary to recall God's design that created the human being masculine and feminine, with a unity and at the same time an original difference and complimentary [sic] ... God entrusts to women and men, according to their respective capacities, a specific vocation and mission in the Church and in the world ... Besides, it is necessary to enable the woman to collaborate in the building of society, appreciating her typical 'feminine genius'.[77]

The most obvious problem with all this is the one that always looms when any group with a power monopoly lays down the law to a powerless group: what one might call the non-representation problem. The Vatican telling women what they are and how they should live is a set of celibate men telling women what to do, when the women have no voice, no tribunal, no right of appeal. The men who are in charge of religion still (with exceptions) appear to find such situations perfectly reasonable and acceptable – and many onlookers fail to be as critical and sceptical as they would of a secular institution that operated that way. The Catholic Church and the Vatican are familiar, they're old news, so we don't bother to point out the absurdities and injustices. But we ought to. It *is* absurd – the male head of an exclusively male hierarchical priesthood, laying down the law to women – all women, women as such – when women have no voice in making the law and no channel of dissent.

Liberal nominal Catholics may ignore Vatican rule-giving – one assumes that Cherie and Tony Blair don't waste much time pondering their fundamental differences – but a great many Catholics are not liberal or nominal, and they don't feel at liberty to disobey; therefore what the Vatican says does matter. The Vatican tells women they are different from men in some significant way, and therefore must live differently and act differently. Women are different so they must limit their ambitions and dreams.

Religions interfere with what is natural all the time. Marriage itself is an interference with nature. So is priestly celibacy. So is the practice of wrapping women in layers of cloth so that men will not be aroused at the sight of them. Religions simply don't as a general rule take what is natural to be a criterion of what is good, so it is not clear why the putative naturalness of female and male sex roles is taken to be such a criterion.

This entire claim that women and men are so different that they must do different kinds of work and live different kinds of lives runs up against the things women and men have been discovering for the past few decades, such as the fact that the vast majority of work in a technological age can be done equally well and easily by either sex. 'Their differences' don't really seem to mean much when it comes to 'collaboration' in the sense of division of labour, especially not in the sense of a mandated or theologically commanded division of labour that applies to everyone regardless of situation and goals and choices. Women can get pregnant, but that is not a reason to restrict what all women are permitted to do. Women can bear and nurse children, but not all of them want to, or do so, and many of those who do, want to devote only a limited amount of time to doing that to the exclusion of everything else. Other than that, 'their differences' do not seem to be such as enforce any particular division of labour. Only women can bear children, but it is not the case that only women can cook or wash clothes or scrub floors or change nappies, nor is it the case that only men can make laws or design buildings or cure diseases or blow things up. The Vatican's insistence on 'difference', like other such insistences, seems like a mere conservative preference for the way things have always been, dressed up as God's preference rather than the Vatican's.

It is even less clear what the new perspectives are that open up for a deeper understanding of the dignity of women, nor what the deeper understanding is, nor what the dignity consists in. As so often with clerical pronouncements, it all just looks like verbiage with no referent.

The dignity of women is in fact just what is being denied or minimized. Permanent consignment to a limited and lesser role in the world is not what 'dignity' is generally understood to mean. The Vatican wouldn't make such assertions about a particular race or nationality – it wouldn't say that black people or aborigines or Indonesians are 'distinct' and will remain so for all eternity, or that their difference is the possibility for collaboration from which new perspectives open up for a deeper understanding of the dignity of black people or aborigines or Indonesians. They wouldn't dare – they know it would bring a hurricane of opprobrium down on their heads, opprobrium of a kind even they don't want to brave.

The Islamic version

Given the clash of civilizations theory, Islamic views on *kufrs*, and recent tensions over the Pope's remarks in Regensburg, it is interesting to see how closely Islam and the Vatican echo each other on the question of women.

Islam has no Vatican or Archbishop of Canterbury; it has only imams and scholars of Islamic law, so fatwas have a more civilian, freelance quality than do papal ordinances or archiepiscopal addresses. Some clerics and 'scholars' build reputations, but there is no single official authority or pinnacle of the hierarchy. Anyone can tell everyone what to do, and many do – and all sound remarkably like the Pope (and of course vice versa).

An article by Maryam Jameelah on feminism and Islam on the popular website Islam 101 cites the views of Syed Hossein Nasr. In *Ideals and Realities of Islam* Nasr says, as clerics always do say, that the family is important – 'the teachings of the *Shariah*' emphasize the role of the family in society: the Muslim family is Muslim society in miniature.

> In it, the man or father functions as the *Imam* in accordance with the patriarchal nature of Islam. The religious responsibility of the family rests upon his shoulders. In the family, the father upholds the tenets of the faith and his authority symbolizes that of God in the world. The man is in fact respected in the family precisely because of the sacerdotal function that he fulfils.[78]

You can't do much better than that. The man functions as the imam, and his authority symbolizes that of God. That clearly puts equality right out of the question, and it makes disobedience or even disagreement a form of blasphemy.

Nasr goes on to say that in rebelling against 'the traditional Muslim family structure' women are rebelling against 'fourteen centuries of Islam itself'. They are few in number but they are 'thirsting for all things Western'. Not quite all – not the dictates of the Vatican, for instance.

From the Islamic point of view, Nasr tells us, discussing the equality of men and women is meaningless.

> It is like discussing the equality of a rose and a jasmine. Each has its own perfume, colour, shape and beauty. Men and women are not the same. Each has particular features and characteristics. Women are not equal to men. But neither are men equal to women. Islam envisages their roles in society not as competing but as complimentary [sic]. Each has certain duties and functions in accordance with his or her nature and constitution.[79]

It isn't very much like discussing the equality of a rose and a jasmine. The jasmine and the rose aren't married; if they were their marriage wouldn't be basic to Muslim society; the rose is not an imam, and the rose's authority does not symbolize that of God. Given all that, the comparison is really very inexact.

In short, it won't do. It won't do to say on one page that the man in the family is the imam and that his authority symbolizes that of God, and on the next page that it is meaningless to discuss equality between men and women. Declaring men imams and their authority symbolic of God's authority is as emphatic and explicit a declaration of inequality between women and men as it is possible to make. With that as the foundation, saying Islam envisages their roles not as competing but as complementary is mere word-juggling.

Nasr then enumerates the many privileges women derive from their inferior, dependent status, such as not having to find husbands for themselves.

> Being able to remain true to her nature, she can afford to sit at home and wait for her parents or guardian to choose a suitable match.[80]

That's one way of putting it. Another way is that she has no option but to sit at home and wait for her parents or guardian to choose a suitable match, and that when her parents or guardian choose a suitable match she may well have no right of refusal.

In exchange for all these putative privileges, Nasr explains, the woman also has responsibilities, the most important being

> to provide a home for her family and to bring up her children properly ... She finds the meaning of her existence in this extended family structure which is constructed so as to give her the maximum possibility of realizing her basic needs and fulfilling herself.
>
> The *Shariah* therefore envisages the role of men and women according to their nature, which is complimentary [sic]. It gives the man the privilege of social and political authority and movement for which he has to pay by bearing heavy responsibilities.[81]

As in the edicts from the Vatican, the Southern Baptists, the Mormons, the Biblical Council, Patrick Henry College – the specific assignments betray the same obdurate fact, however earnestly the clerics insist otherwise. Men have the privilege of social and political authority, and women don't. It's useless to say that is 'complementary' rather than unequal: unequal is exactly what it is.

Rafia Zakaria, a graduate student at Indiana University, points out the problem.

> American law says men and women are equal, whereas Muslim religious texts say they 'complement' each other, Ms. Zakaria said. 'If the law says they are equal, it's hard to see how in their spiritual lives they will accept a whole different identity.'[82]

IslamOnline is a popular source for fatwas. It reads like a pious version of Dear Abby or Miss Manners – readers send in questions, and mullahs provide the answers. One question was about women leading Friday prayers; Sheikh Muhammad Nur Abdullah, President of the Islamic Society of North American and member of the Fiqh Council of North America, answered:

> There is a consensus among Muslim jurists that a woman is not allowed to lead men in a Mosque or congregation. Also, she is not allowed to lead people in a Friday Prayer or to deliver the Friday *khutbah*. She is, however, allowed to lead a congregation consisting only of women.[83]

Sheikh Yusuf al-Qaradawi discussed the question at more length:

> Throughout Muslim history it has never been heard of a woman leading the Friday Prayer or delivering the Friday sermon, even during the era when a woman, Shagarat Ad-Durr, was ruling the Muslims in Egypt during the Mamluk period.
>
> It is established that leadership in Prayer in Islam is to be for men. People praying behind an imam are to follow him in the movements of prayer – bowing, prostrating, etc., and listen attentively to him reciting the Qur'an in Prayer.
>
> Prayer in Islam is an act that involves different movements of the body; it does not consist merely of saying supplications as it is the case with prayer in Christianity. Moreover, it requires concentration of the mind, humility, and complete submission of the heart to Almighty Allah. Hence, it does not befit a woman, whose structure of physique naturally arouses instincts in men, to lead men in Prayer and stand in front of them, for this may divert the men's attention from concentrating in the Prayer and the spiritual atmosphere required.
>
> ...
>
> Rulings pertaining to leadership in Prayer are established by evidence of authentic hadiths as well as the scholarly unanimity of Muslims. They are based on religious teachings, not on social customs as it is has been claimed.
>
> The different juristic schools agree that it is not permissible for women to lead men in the obligatory Prayer, though some scholars voice the opinion that the woman who is well-versed in the Qur'an may lead the members of her family, including men, in Prayer on the basis that there is no room for stirring instincts in this case.[84]

This, to be quite frank, is frivolous. Women have a 'structure of physique' which arouses instincts in men, therefore only men can lead men (and women) in prayer, therefore all clerics in Islam must be male, therefore all interpretation and enforcement of rules must be done by men, therefore women are subject to strictures and limitations that reach into all corners of their lives, while having no voice or representation. That won't do. It's not a serious reason for such a radical subordination.

The reason is also self-servingly circular. Men were in charge when Islam was established, so men kept men in charge, so men are still in charge, so men are in a position to say 'women distract men so they can't participate'. It's a loop with no exit. Women could make the same claim, but they have no standing to make any claims, so that is beside the point. The clergy is male, scholars are male, judges are male, so it is always men who rule that women are intended for domestic duty first and foremost.

> It is important here to state that the original judgment concerning acts of worship is that anything not prescribed in Shari'ah in explicit texts is prohibited, so that people may not innovate matters in religion not ordained by Allah. Thus, people may not innovate a certain act of worship, change or add things in the ordained ones according to their own fancies or only because they think such matters are desirable. Whoever innovates anything in religion or adds to it whatever is not in it – that addition or innovation is rejected.[85]

Also from IslamOnline:

> First of all, it should be clear that the Qur'an and the Prophet's Sunnah bear witness to the fact that woman is at least as vital to life as man himself, and that she is not inferior to him. When the Shari'ah restricts some positions to men, it does not mean discrimination, but this should be understood within the frame of the general objectives of the Shari'ah, which are set by the Law-giver (Almighty Allah) to order the lives of men and women in a way that best suits their natures.[86]

It is striking how unconvincing all this is. Granted, it is largely addressed to people who already accept it, or who are primed to feel duty-bound to accept whatever the institution tells them, but the perfunctory quality of the reasoning behind the rules still comes as a surprise. A combination of chapter and verse and a mere gesture at a secular utilitarian reason seems to be all that's thought necessary. Timothy 2:11–15 plus family harmony. It's not much on which to base the subordination of more than half of humanity.

Equally striking is the way the rules and rulings attempt to accommodate modernity at the same time as they repudiate it. They defend a reactionary view of sex roles and of women's capabilities and wants, but in the same breath they disavow the reactionary underpinnings of those views. It's not that they consider women not equal (let alone inferior – that word isn't even spoken); it's that they consider them different. Equality, the imams and priests solemnly repeat, does not mean sameness. No, to be sure, it doesn't, but it does generally mean sameness of treatment, sameness of laws, sameness of opportunities, sameness of rights. What it does not mean – what it is generally taken to *rule out* – is instruction from the authorities on what kind of work one can and cannot attempt, what kind of life one can and cannot choose. We no longer believe groups of people are born to do this and not that, to take their instructions from strangers making generalizations about them and then to accept limits on their aspirations set by people in privileged positions. The modern world has (with much struggle and effort) moved on from that way of arranging things. Conservative clerics are fighting a rearguard action against that move, using their one crude weapon of 'difference'.

The difference in question is the old familiar one that is dubbed 'natural' – women are domestic and men are public; women raise children and serve husbands, men go into the world and make money. There is a vast literature on how natural all this is or is not, and on which parts of it are natural and which are social, but in any case it is a truism that what is natural is not necessarily what is moral or useful or healthy or optimal in any way. Disease is natural, starvation is natural, high infant mortality is natural, drought is natural, floods are natural; that doesn't make any of them desirable. The vicars and bishops and mullahs who issue fiats about the natural division of labour between the sexes also drive cars, sleep in beds, use electric lights and refrigerators and computers, watch TV and play music, read and write, wear clothes, take medicine. They don't urge step-fathers to murder their step-children, which in many primate and other species is natural. Their valorization of the natural as the right is highly selective, even idiosyncratic, since so much of clerical morality is about, precisely, *not* doing what is natural. It is not obvious why putative 'natural' differences between the sexes make the one exception to this rule.

Behind the mask

There is also of course the faint hum of deception in the background. All of these clerical pronouncements claim, indeed insist, that the woman's allotted role is just as valuable and significant as the man's. It is different, but certainly not inferior; different, but equal – just as the woman is (oh certainly) equal, but different. But is anyone convinced?

It is difficult to be convinced when the role allotted to men is the one where all the real power and influence are. It cannot be seen as a mere coincidence that consigning women to family, home, the domestic, and allowing men the world, the public, people at large, gives men much larger opportunities to make things happen, and also gives them the power to go on consigning women to family, home, the domestic.

The world is where laws are made and interpreted and enforced, wars are fought, things are made and bought and sold, research is done, knowledge is collected and shared, opinion is shaped; where people are governed, employed, taught, trained, rewarded, punished, healed, challenged. The world is where the interesting stuff happens.

The world is where people deal with other people, in wholesale lots; where people deal with large numbers of strangers. Home is where people deal with other people they know well, one or two or three at a time. Home is miniature; the world is large. The smallness and intimacy and relatedness of home are fine things, but not if one is confined to them permanently.

The fact that the world is where the laws and rules and norms are made also means that a sexual division of the two entails that women are subject to laws and rules and norms that they have no part in making. The conflict of interest is inescapable. It is men who allot men the realm where the rules are laid down, and they lay down rules that allot them the realm where the rules are laid down. This won't do. It's an old and familiar pattern, of course. The nobility or monarchy or oligarchy or military junta or clergy make rules that place all power in their hands, and thus minority rule is perpetuated indefinitely. Gentiles make bylaws excluding Jews, and naturally Jews have no say in the matter. Slave-owners write a constitution which excludes slaves from citizenship. Male clerics write rules stipulating that clerics must be male. It's an old pattern, but hardly a just one, and it's been steadily eroding for at least two centuries. Religion is perhaps the only institution left that's still willing to try it on.

The reality is that it's difficult if not impossible to declare people systematically different without implicitly declaring them inferior. That's why laws in many places have been gradually changing to reflect this for at least a century. In the USA, for instance, the notorious 1896 Supreme Court decision in Plessy v Ferguson accepted the principle (or the legal fiction) of separate but equal. It took more than half a century, but in 1954 another Supreme Court decision, Brown v Board of Education of Topeka, overturned Plessy and ruled that separate could not be equal.

So with laws and religious edicts concerning women. It won't do to claim that a division of labour which confines women to the domestic and allows men the whole world is mere difference or mere separation. The reasons are not difficult to see. The first that jumps out is that domestic work is unskilled work, while it is skilled work that commands respect, status, power and money. If women are suited or fitted or destined for domestic work alone, by implication they are not suited for work that requires learning and skill. That is a workable definition of 'inferior'.

By the same token, rules and edicts that allow men but not women full access to the world and what is done there necessarily imply that this reflects their respective abilities and talents. If men are capable of working in government, law, education, administration, engineering, medicine, design, construction, manufacturing, and women are not, then it is tactful but absurd to claim this is *mere* difference as opposed to *qualitative* difference.

Moreover, the separation – the 'difference' or 'complementarity' – that the edicts command cause real-world effects as well as ideological ones. If there is such a clear separation (as there was in the past, and still is in much of the world, and could be anywhere again), then all the worldly institutions are staffed by men, their rules and customs are made by men, their decisions and policies are the work of men, their hiring and promotion are overseen by men. A vicious circle is created by which women are excluded from vocations X Y and Z by rules they have no part in making, so the arrangement simply becomes perpetual, as Mill pointed out a century and a half ago.

> For, what is the peculiar character of the modern world – the difference which chiefly distinguishes modern institutions, modern social ideas, modern life itself, from those of times long past? It is, that human beings are no longer born to their place in life, and chained down by an inexorable bond to the place they are born to, but are free to employ their faculties, and such favourable chances as offer, to achieve the lot which may appear to them most desirable. Human society of old was constituted on a very different principle. All were born to a fixed social position, and were mostly kept in it by law, or interdicted from any means by which they could emerge from it. As some men are born white and others black, so some were born slaves and others freemen and citizens; some were born patricians, others plebeians; some were born feudal nobles, others commoners and roturiers ... In modern Europe, and most in those parts of it which have participated most largely in all other modern improvements, diametrically opposite doctrines now prevail. Law and government do not undertake to prescribe by whom any social or industrial operation shall or shall not be conducted, or what modes of conducting them shall be lawful. These things are left to the unfettered choice of individuals ... The old theory was, that the least possible should be left to the choice of the individual agent; that all he had to do should,

as far as practicable, be laid down for him by superior wisdom. Left to himself he was sure to go wrong. The modern conviction, the fruit of a thousand years of experience, is, that things in which the individual is the person directly interested, never go right but as they are left to his own discretion; and that any regulation of them by authority, except to protect the rights of others, is sure to be mischievous … It is not that all processes are supposed to be equally good, or all persons to be equally qualified for everything; but that freedom of individual choice is now known to be the only thing which procures the adoption of the best processes, and throws each operation into the hands of those who are best qualified for it. Nobody thinks it necessary to make a law that only a strong-armed man shall be a blacksmith … In consonance with this doctrine, it is felt to be an overstepping of the proper bounds of authority to fix beforehand, on some general presumption, that certain persons are not fit to do certain things. It is now thoroughly known and admitted that if some such presumptions exist, no such presumption is infallible. Even if it be well grounded in a majority of cases, which it is very likely not to be, there will be a minority of exceptional cases in which it does not hold: and in those it is both an injustice to the individuals, and a detriment to society, to place barriers in the way of their using their faculties for their own benefit and for that of others … At present, in the more improved countries, the disabilities of women are the only case, save one, in which laws and institutions take persons at their birth, and ordain that they shall never in all their lives be allowed to compete for certain things. The one exception is that of royalty.[87]

It is noticeable that clerics don't in fact attempt to rule on who should do which jobs in general. It is noticeable that this vocational stipulation applies *only* to women. Mainstream clerics no longer claim that blacks or Jews or foreigners or natives are fitted only for unskilled work. It is only women who are told that they are 'naturally fitted' to do one kind of work to the exclusion of all others. It is interesting to note that the first is no longer socially acceptable while the second is.

There is an odd sort of impertinence about this sort of thing. It's like reading a sixteenth-century homily telling everyone how to act towards superiors, how to dress, how to talk, how to live. We no longer expect the authorities to tell us what to do in such a detailed, minute, searching way – but religion is the exception to that. Possibly that is one of the chief remaining purposes of religion: to offer people a pretext for issuing orders to everyone else. Those who want to command everyone to live according to a particular conservative idea of tradition have the fig leaf of clerical authority to cover their intrusiveness. No one but clerics would dare lay down the law in such an unabashed way.

The godly woman

In August 2007 the Southwestern Baptist Theological Seminary was in the news over its plan to introduce a bachelor of arts in humanities degree in 'homemaking' that would be open only to women. The Seminary's President, Paige Patterson, said at the convention's annual meeting that year that 'We are moving against the tide in order to establish family and gender roles as described in God's word for the home and the family.'[88] The seminary's website introduces the programme this way:

> The College at Southwestern endeavors to prepare women to model the characteristics of the godly woman as outlined in Scripture. This is accomplished through instruction in homemaking skills, developing insights into home and family while continuing to equip women to understand and engage the culture of today.[89]

A reporter for the *Los Angeles Times* found that as of the first semester only eight of the three hundred undergraduates at the seminary were enrolled in the homemaking concentration, but that many more women study traditional gender roles in courses such as 'Wife of the Equipping Minister'. At a session of the latter one woman talked about her hobby of cross-stitching, another showed how she uses the internet to track grocery coupons, and a third 'drew excited murmurs with her talk on meal planning, featuring a recipe for a sure-fire "freezer pleaser" – a triple batch of meatloaf (secret ingredient: oatmeal)'. Then for the rest of the class the wife of a theology professor 'laid out the biblical basis for what she calls "the glorious inequalities of life" '.

> [Ashley] Smith, 30, confided that she sometimes resents her husband for advancing his career 'while I'm changing diapers and getting poop all over me.' But then she quoted from Ephesians: 'Wives, submit to your own husbands, as to the Lord.' And from Genesis: God created Eve to be a 'suitable helper' for Adam.
>
> 'If we love the Scripture, we must do it,' said Smith, who gave up her dreams of a career when her husband said it was time to have children. 'We must fit into this role. It's so much more important than our own personal happiness.'[90]

So this is what all the talk of equal but different, of complementarity, of women's special role, comes down to – grown women in a university classroom studying supermarket coupons and meat loaf. So this is what 'graciously submitting' and 'the fundamental human capacity to live for the other' mean: adult women concerning themselves with trivia – dressing up trivia as something worth intellectual attention. It's like a sort of insulting masquerade: as if the (real) grownups had conspired to trick them, or placate them, by disguising their mudpie-making as an academic discipline – allowing them to sit in classrooms and write in notebooks and play at Going To University.

The blunt truth is that (whether they realize it or not) these women are collaborating in their own infantilization.

There is also the risible disconnect between meat loaf and coupons, and the Bible.

> Seminary President Paige Patterson and his wife, Dorothy – who goes by Mrs. Paige Patterson – view the homemaking curriculum as a way to spread the Christian faith.
>
> In their vision, graduates will create such gracious homes that strangers will take note.[91]

The Southern Baptist Convention, as we have seen, declared in 1998 that a wife should 'graciously submit' herself to her husband's leadership; Paige Patterson wrote that statement. One can't help suspecting that the word 'gracious' and its cognates are an important part of the Patterson household idiolect. Wendy Wasserstein in her play *Uncommon Women and Others* made ironic use of Mount Holyoke College's tradition of 'gracious living' – apparently a matter of white gloves and tea twice a week. The tradition, needless to say, passed into desuetude decades ago.

What Ashley Smith calls 'Scripture' is not the Bible; it's *Father Knows Best* or *Leave it to Beaver* or *The Donna Reed Show*; it's nostalgia for a TV-sitcom-shaped idea of 1950s Family Life, in which Dad goes to Work every day and Mom makes Cookies and the Kids get into Mischief. It's a fantasy of The Way We Never Were[92] which is very time-specific, very local, very wealth- and technology-dependent, and very difficult to find in the Bible.

In short the Southern Baptists are rather obviously confusing their fondness for a simple-minded idea of what American family life was like fifty years ago with a putative Christian idea of family life. The Vatican, with only slightly more sophisticated rhetoric, does much the same thing (though presumably without the memory of old US sitcoms).

And after the mountain has laboured and brought forth a mouse, what is the result? Ashley Smith abdicates the right to live the life she would have preferred, because she loves 'the Scripture'.

God's plan for his Church

It is not completely obvious why clerics have the kind of moral authority they do have. It's a long tradition, and habit is powerful, but humans have cast off other traditions and habits. However that may be, clerics do have moral authority for many people: they are understood to have a right and a duty to tell people how to live and what to be. Given that that is the case, it seems very desirable that at a minimum they should follow rules that apply to the rest of society. If nothing else, they should not give themselves permission to exclude half of humanity from their ranks, *and at the same time* lay down rules for that half of humanity.

Viewed from this angle, the significance of the ordination of women is not so much the inclusion of women as it is the anomaly and non-representation of an all-male clergy. To put it as starkly as possible, if clerics are going to tell women what to do, they have no right to exclude them from their ranks. If they insist on doing that, then their rule-giving should be dismissed as the self-serving homiletics of an interested party, like a factory owner lecturing workers on the value of hard work and thrift.

Meanwhile, however, this absurd situation is exactly the one that persists. Male clerics who lecture women on complementarity do indeed exclude women from their ranks, on the grounds that women have always been excluded from the clergy.

Predictably, John Paul II was firmly opposed to the ordination of women.

> Priestly ordination, which hands on the office entrusted by Christ to his Apostles of teaching, sanctifying and governing the faithful, has in the Catholic Church from the beginning always been reserved to men alone. This tradition has also been faithfully maintained by the Oriental Churches.
>
> When the question of the ordination of women arose in the Anglican Communion, Pope Paul VI, out of fidelity to his office of safeguarding the Apostolic Tradition, and also with a view to removing a new obstacle placed in the way of Christian unity, reminded Anglicans of the position of the Catholic Church: 'She holds that it is not admissible to ordain women to the priesthood, for very fundamental reasons. These reasons include: the example recorded in the Sacred Scriptures of Christ choosing his Apostles only from among men; the constant practice of the Church, which has imitated Christ in choosing only men; and her living teaching authority which has consistently held that the exclusion of women from the priesthood is in accordance with God's plan for his Church.'[93]

Again, these very fundamental reasons seem surprisingly feeble. They are doubtless convincing to believers – or perhaps they simply fall in with and fail to disturb the settled habits and customs of believers – but to outsiders they seem naked. Christ chose his apostles only from men. He also presumably chose them only from Aramaic-speakers, only from Judeans, only from Jews. He probably also chose them from working people, from people with little education, from people who hadn't seen much of the world. He chose them from people who shared a great many variables that have never been criteria for the priesthood. It is not self-evident why being a man is the one salient variable when one is trying to imitate Christ.

A more rational explanation would be that women were excluded from non-domestic work as much as possible, but less than 100 per cent; there were some exceptions, but jobs with real power over other people, especially men, were more firmly closed to women than other jobs were, because in a context in which women are an emphatically subordinated group, men find it intensely degrading and unmanning to be told what to do by a woman. It's reasonable to think that if Jesus chose his apostles he chose all men because that was the obvious, default thing to do, the path of least resistance, so that it didn't rise to the level of a decision at all. There is little reason to think he intended the maleness of the apostles to be a binding precedent for all future clerics in a church that didn't exist. Their other commonalities – regional origin, language group, nationality, education level, work history – are not taken to be binding precedents, so it is not at all clear why their maleness should be. Such careful cherry-picking of relevant factors can't help but look self-serving.

And the objection is almost too obvious to be worth making. Of course they were all men, because that was normal, which is exactly why reformist movements want to change that. It's simply obtuse to meet an attempt at reformist opening-up of opportunities by pointing out the very exclusion that is at issue. Galen and Hippocrates were men; it doesn't follow that all doctors ought to be men forever after.

The same objections apply to the imitation of Christ claim, and the final item is simply obscurantism. The 'living teaching authority' is simply a way of dignifying dogmatism. The claim that the putative living teaching authority is in accordance with God's plan for his Church is simply dogmatism undisguised. There is no evidence that God has a plan for the Church, nor is there any evidence that the Church has any genuine knowledge of such a plan. It is all assertion.

None of this is in the least surprising, but it is worth pointing out, since in fact the Church does use these unsupported assertions as if they were genuine knowledge and reasonable arguments. It is worth pointing out their fundamental hollowness.

This is all the more true because such hollow arguments would no longer work in any secular enterprise, and it is not clear why mere non-secularism should justify deference for empty claims. No company or professional organization could now get away with saying it is not admissible to hire women for the key jobs because the founder gave all the key jobs to men, or that the exclusion of women from the key jobs is in accordance with the founder's plan for his organization. Nor could it get away with saying it is not admissible to hire women for the key jobs because God made women and men different – that would be not only socially unacceptable, but also against the law.

Religion is different, it may be objected. Religion is vital to people, it is part of their identity, it needs special protection. In the USA, the First Amendment to the Constitution explicitly gives it special protection in the free exercise clause (at the cost of much controversy). How much special protection religious institutions should have is a contentious issue, to put it mildly; but at the very least it seems both reasonable and necessary to point out the weakness of its arguments.

The trouble here is that until very recently, almost all jobs had always 'been reserved to men alone'. There came a time when enough women became tired of seeing all jobs reserved to men alone that they began to agitate and campaign to get some jobs unreserved, and then more, and more, up until the present. That is how social change often works: things have always (at least as far as anyone knows) been a certain way, and then people who are excluded or disadvantaged or exploited under that arrangement decide to try to change it. Workers form unions, civil rights activists get laws and customs changed, and so on. Precedent is not necessarily considered a good reason to continue as before, because it is the precedent itself that is being questioned. In that light it is rather futile for the Pope to tell the Anglican Church that ordination has always been reserved to men alone when the church knows that perfectly well and when that very monopoly is just what it wants to end. It would have been similarly futile for a state official in Mississippi to tell a roomful of civil rights workers that 'we have always treated nigras like dirt in Mississippi' in the expectation that that would cause them to give up and go home.

It's too late for that now. The genie is out of the bottle. We know now that people aren't born with fixed destinies or roles or life plans. We know that divisions of labour are arrangements, not biological essences. We know that people have different aptitudes, interests, hopes, and that it makes no sense for State or Church to decide ahead of time what people should do in life according to what *group* they belong to. We know that it's the business of individuals to decide what they want to do with their lives, and the business of parents to decide how they want to split up child-rearing duties. Priests and imams, ministers and rabbis can still lay down the law, but they can't conceal the fact that millions of women around the world refuse to be 'for the home' as opposed to the world, or submissive to a husband. Clerical insistence that women are destined for smaller more obedient lives is a pustular pocket of injustice in the world, and has to be exposed and resisted.

4 Honour Is Between the Legs of Women

Needless to say, the kitchen is not the only room in the house, and women are not wanted only for their ability to cook or raise crops. Their primary duty is sexual, and it is that very fact that makes them such a risk. Because their primary duty is sexual, their mere presence is a danger-magnet, an aperture in the house through which other men can enter and violate the resident man. A woman is like a piece of meat calling to all the cats and dogs in the vicinity, like a bleeding thrashing fish in a pool of sharks. The thing about her that is of most value to the man makes her also a lure for all other men, so a man makes himself vulnerable to theft and shame and dishonour by possession of the thing he most wants.

In short, a woman in the house necessarily carries with her the possibility that other men can have sex with her; this is a brute physical fact and so it becomes a psychological and social one. Women create an opening for shame for whichever man owns them; for their husbands above all, and in the interim before they have husbands, for their fathers, who own them until the husbands take over (a fact vividly illustrated by the wedding custom in which the father 'gives away' the bride).

In a way it might seem odd for a father to bother about a future husband who isn't yet anyone in particular, but there is a sort of quid pro quo in effect, a freemasonry as it were, in which men anxiously protect the rights of men in general to the combination of guaranteed access and monopoly. A man who has an unmarried daughter has a duty to the male community to adhere to the rules that protect the monopoly–access combination. The enjoyment of monopoly access creates the obligation to protect the principle of monopoly access. Employers protect their interests, workers protect theirs: self-interest and solidarity interconnect. (This is one reason for men in patriarchal cultures not to *want* daughters: because of this fearsome risk and responsibility and potential for shame and failure.)

Thus the brute physical and social fact means that fathers and brothers are vulnerable to violation by external men as long as an unmarried daughter is living in the house, and thus that they are obligated to block access to her genitals by whatever means necessary. Once she is married this fraught responsibility passes to her husband, who at least gets the reward of unmetered sex. But then of course he also runs the risk of having a daughter himself and being saddled with the anxious and unrewarded duty of blocking access to *her* genitals. Life is never easy.

In more liberal, egalitarian cultures this worry is managed in more or less mild ways – via love and loyalty, customs and rules, promises and commitments, all of which can and frequently do break down, creating the stuff of novels and pop songs and movies. The overall default expectation, however, is something more like a social contract than a prison sentence or indentured servitude. Sensible parents raise their daughters to be at least aware of the risk of pregnancy and STDs, and perhaps to postpone the complications of sex until they're old enough to deal with them – a malleable age which depends on the parents, the daughters, local mores, and other imponderables. Couples negotiate sexual fidelity, or not, and they keep their promises, or they don't; but either way they generally take on the inherent risks rather than trying to make the female half of the couple physically inaccessible at all times.

In terms of human history, however, more liberal, egalitarian cultures are a novelty; in terms of geography and demographics, they're still a rarity. The *norm*, in both time and space, is male dominance and female subservience. The attempt to eradicate the power imbalance between women and men could be seen as a naïve, eccentric aberration of decadent late-modern Westerners – were it not for long experience and abundant evidence of the way people bloom and flourish when granted rights and responsibilities. The fact remains, however, that cultures which are now more or less egalitarian and liberal certainly haven't always been so, and that women have been sequestered, veiled, chaperoned, restricted in most places through most of history. They have also, however, complained and protested, and in fortunate regions egalitarian ideas kept inexorably spreading until they finally encompassed even women, even slaves, even homosexuals. The result is more uncertainty but less resentment, which seems a pretty good bargain.

A good bargain, but not by any means a universal one. Where the bargain hasn't been struck, the arrangement is the old one of forcible concealment and restraint accompanied by permanent simmering suspicion, anxiety and hostility.

The suspicion and anxiety are rooted not just in worries about sexual infidelity on its own, but also in the additional brute physical fact that if a woman has sex with another man she can get pregnant by the other man, without her husband's knowledge, and thus he can be tricked into wasting his resources raising another man's child (as well as delaying conception of his own). In selfish gene terms this is a heavy cost.

However, humans can change or get around many brute physical facts by means of technology. There's certainly a technological fix for the dreaded possibility of the woman accidentally getting pregnant by the wrong man: reliable contraception prevents unintended consequences of that kind, and thus, if used, can remove the grounds for much of the male mistrust of the female. The technological fix, however, works only for unintended pregnancy; if a woman actually wants to get pregnant by another man, we're back where we started. In any case custom, religion, opinion, feeling can take a very long time to catch up with technology. To many people (including many in secular industrialized countries) the fact that contraception could free women to be something more than baby factories, *and* could enable them to have non-marital sex without detection or consequences, is not a liberation but a downward plunge into chaos and wickedness. To many people women are *meant* – by God – to be wives and mothers and *nothing else*, and any technology or ideas or laws that would alter that are the spawn of the Devil.

However that may be, before the technology of birth control was improved and so became reliable, cheap, and more or less easy (though greater ease tended to entail worse side effects – for the woman), the only way to deal with the intolerable risks of the impregnatable woman was thought to be ferocious control. Control of the woman, that is – control of the impregnator was never really seriously considered an option. Sermons on concupiscence were all right, but actual restriction of men's liberties, or even much in the way of social consequences, were not seen as a viable solution. We leave it to the reader to ponder the likely reasons.

All of this is of course about the logic of domination and of the biological basis for sexual control. Real life is less stark and more complicated, and there will always be exceptions. Nevertheless, the reality is often more exceptionless and harsh than outsiders can readily imagine.

One woman's experience

Carmen Bin Ladin was born and raised in Switzerland, the daughter of an Iranian (or Persian, as CBL prefers to call her) mother and Swiss father. She met Yeslam Bin Ladin when he and his mother and siblings spent a summer in Geneva in 1973; the two fell in love and agreed to marry.

On her first, brief trip to Saudi Arabia in 1974, for her marriage, CBL was uncomfortable in her *abaya* and stunned by the 'almost hypnotic inactivity' of female life. Only men could come and go as they pleased; women were confined to the house. They took no exercise, because walking anywhere was completely unthinkable.

> At first I wasn't even aware of what seemed so strange about this country, but then it hit me: Half the population of Saudi Arabia is kept behind walls, all the time. It was hard to fathom, a city with almost no women. I felt like a ghost: Women didn't exist, in this world of men.[1]

The two moved to Jeddah in 1976. Carmen was uneasy about having to wear an *abaya* and about all the other restrictions, but she thought Saudi society would modernize just as other cultures had. Soon, as in Iran, the veil would be something women could choose to wear, or not; women would be able to walk around the streets, drive, shop on their own, work. Meanwhile she had to adjust to things as they were.

The hardest part was becoming absorbed into her mother-in-law's quiet slow life, her woman's world; it was like going under an anaesthetic. Om Yeslam's only interests were cooking and the Koran; 'she lived in a world that was strictly bound by an invisible cage of tradition.'[2] Every minute of her life was ruled by the rituals and rules of Islamic custom. Everything seemed to be *haram*, sinful, except when it was *abe*, shameful. Music was *haram*, walking in the street was *abe*, being seen by a man was *haram*, talking to a male servant was *abe*. The system constricted all women in a mesh of restraints that made daily life maddeningly complicated as well as stultifyingly empty. Women weren't allowed to shop, so servants had to bring goods home for approval until the right items were found. CBL needed Similac (formula milk) for her baby daughter, and the servants couldn't find any, so she finally insisted on going to the grocery store herself. Her husband and driver took her there, '*abaya*-ed from head to toe', and had her wait in the car for ten minutes while the entire staff and all the customers evacuated the store.

> What on earth did they fear – contamination? From one woman, whose face and body could not even be seen? Could it really be a sign of

politeness and respect for these men to turn their backs on me because I was a woman?[3]

Her husband's sister Fawzia was studying business at the university, but her 'classes' were actually video presentations by male professors who could not teach directly in a strictly segregated classroom. Women students could not use the library, but had to apply for books in writing and pick them up at an office a week later. CBL never saw Fawzia read a book and never heard her talk about her studies. The boredom and aimlessness of her life made CBL feel stifled.[4]

Her husband's father, Sheikh Mohamed, the patriarch who had amassed a fortune in construction and was in charge of the maintenance of the holy sites in Mecca and Medina, had 22 wives and 54 children (one of the younger sons of course being Osama). He had total power over all his wives; he could neglect them or divorce them at will, while they lived in confinement, completely dependent on him and in awe of him. 'I rarely met a Saudi woman,' CBL notes, 'who was not afraid of her husband.'[5] A wife in Saudi Arabia can do nothing without her husband's permission; women there live in obedience, isolation, and fear of being summarily divorced.

The lives of the women in the Bin Laden family were so constrained, so small and faded, that it frightened her. They never left their houses alone, they never did anything; their only goal seemed to be to follow more perfectly the most restrictive rules of Islam. They were kept like pets by their husbands, shut up at home and occasionally taken out for a treat. They never read anything but the Koran, never saw men other than their husbands, never talked about larger issues with anyone. They had nothing to say, and they bored CBL to tears. She clutched at every sign that Saudi Arabia was modernizing – a lifted veil on the street, a women-only bank, a bookstore – but only to be disappointed. The bookstore had almost no books: customs officials excluded books by Jews and most other books as well.[6]

In 1978 one of the king's great-nieces, Princess Mish'al, was shot to death in a car park. She had been promised in marriage to a much older man, had tried to leave the country with her lover, and had been captured at the airport. Her grandfather, Prince Mohamed, ordered her killed for bringing shame on her family. CBL was rigid with horror. Her first thought was for her daughters. One of their uncles might be perfectly capable of ordering his niece to be put to death. 'And I would be powerless. There are no words to describe my anger and my renewed panic that day.'[7]

And as her daughters grew older, things got harder. They were living in a society 'where women were nothing, and wanted to be nothing'. CBL felt frustrated, surrounded by women who didn't have the will to resist. 'They lived, but only for their faith; their personalities were completely annihilated.'[8] Saudi children are trained, from very young, to adhere to a strict code; women's inferior status and subservience is bred into their bones. Little girls know they are required to walk, dress and talk unobtrusively, and to be submissive, docile and obedient.[9]

CBL began to dread her eldest daughter's first period, at which point she could no longer delay wearing the *abaya*. CBL tried to reason with herself – she wore the *abaya*, it wasn't so terrible, merely inconvenient … but she no longer felt confident that one day her daughters would be able to choose not to wear it if they wanted to. Suddenly her own silver-embroidered *abaya* looked hideous to her, and she realized she was shaping her daughters into women who would rebel from a society that wanted to lock them in. Princess Mish'al's murder had shown that rebellious women could be marked for death. 'In my nightmares I saw my little girls growing up to become Saudi women – bent over under the weight of their subservience, cloaked in darkness.'[10]

That's the horror; that's what CBL didn't want, for herself and, passionately, for her daughters: being emptied out until nothing is left and nothing matters, until the personality is annihilated.

The point here isn't that women are necessarily actively unhappy when they are subordinated and without rights; some may not be. It is something much more profound: that they've been too limited, stunted, distorted, emptied out, even to *be* unhappy – they've been made nothing.

The subordination of women is in this way like slavery, and serfdom, and untouchability, and proletarianization. If a set of people are rigorously limited from birth – then they may accept their lot; they may be tame, docile, subservient, 'reliable' – but only at the price of not being fully human.

It may be the most basic commitment of modern secular rights-based liberalism, that *no one* should ever be prevented from being fully human; *no one* should be stunted and limited from birth.

The Saudi government has in place a system which requires every Saudi woman to have a male guardian, a husband or father, son or brother, uncle or cousin, who makes decisions for her on all sorts of matters. Adult women have to get permission from a male guardian to work, travel, attend university or marry. Women are not allowed to make decisions for their children, even trivial ones. Male guardianship is nearly impossible to remove, even from violent or abusive guardians.[11]

Sex segregation is strictly enforced in Saudi Arabia, and makes it impossible for Saudi women to take any part in public life. Segregation does not generally translate to separate facilities for women and men, but rather, almost always means facilities for men only, and nothing for women.

Ferocious control

The felt need for ferocious control, and many of the ways that control is maintained, have survived into the time after the development of easier, more reliable contraception. A Saudi woman could be medically sterile, she could be post-hysterectomy, but that would make no difference to the restrictions that govern her life. Some restrictions are slightly loosened for women over 45, but younger women can't be *seen* to be sterile, and appearance is everything. The felt need for control has survived as an independent self-justifying self-perpetuating imperative. For whatever reason – out of force of habit, tradition, honour, shame, culture, piety, jealousy, love of power, love of bullying – it is still taken for granted in many places that men may roam the world freely, wear jeans and T-shirts, and do as they like, but that women must be subject to a myriad of special rules; that they must be confined, hidden, forbidden to do many things at all and allowed to do others only with the permission of a male relative. It is still taken for granted in many places, in short, that men should be treated like adults and women should be treated like children.

One consequence is a loss of productivity and hence of economic development and prosperity, and thus, probably, of opportunities for liberal democracy and equal rights, leading to continued loss of productivity, etcetera, in a loop of futility. This also helps to explain the widespread preference for male children. Girls are hampered from birth: kept out of school entirely or taken out early, fed less, married off at an early age; they are not in a position to help their parents. Add to this the fact that most girls marry out, that many require an expensive dowry on marriage, and that girls are seen as a potential source of dishonour and shame. With all this, women become a tragedy of the commons: most men want to have their own woman, but many parents don't want to have and raise girl children. Women are necessary, but it should always be someone else who does the grim work of actually producing them. *They* must have the daughters; we want to have all sons, and we want all of them to have all sons too.

Now that pre-natal sex testing is possible, and not only possible but widely available, the someone else approach is no longer just a wish; it can be put into practice, and it often is.[12] The result, however, is not increased valuation of women, but increased coercion and violence. Where women are scarce, the result is not better treatment but more abduction, forced marriage, and rape. Heads I win tails you lose.

All but one

The control of women is dual. The goal is to deny access to the woman's genitals to all men in the world minus one *and* to guarantee access to one. Neither aspect is at all optional or negotiable or subject to the woman's will or choice or permission. It's not about what the woman wants, or what she might need, or what is best for her. It's about the man who owns her, and no one else.

The first part of this is familiar enough. We know women are (more or less, depending on local customs) expected to be monogamous, and that they're more expected to be monogamous than men are. We know about the double standards. But the second part is somewhat less familiar. That's doubtless partly because it's largely superfluous in cultures where marriage, love and sex are voluntary even for women; where women are allowed to choose their lovers or husbands, and also whether or not to have sex with them on any particular occasion (so allowed that 'not tonight, dear, I have a headache' has been a stock joke for generations). The ability and right to refuse all along the line – to refuse to marry, to refuse an unwanted man, to refuse to have sex at any particular moment – underlies the ability to accept. The two march together. Where people are able to choose their own marriage partners, and their time of marriage, and when to have sex, they don't need to be coerced. (The ability to refuse means some people will be disappointed, but their best option is not to use force but to watch Oprah or get a makeover or read some self-help books.) Most people who have grown up in liberal secular societies fail to realize how taken for granted it is elsewhere that girls and women have no rights over their own genitals or their own lives.

In patriarchal cultures or enclaves, however, this idea is familiar, and crucial. There women and their genitals are a natural resource, like fertile cropland, good planting weather, a seam of coal. They are something that *must not* be wasted; they are there to be *used*. What they may want is no more to the point than what an unploughed field or an uncut forest may want. Women don't own their bodies, they are merely tenants; the owner is always male, a father or husband or son or brother, or failing that a more distant male relative. The woman's genitals are his property, to sell or barter as he sees fit.[13]

One religious sect that makes this almost risibly unmistakable is not in Saudi Arabia or Pakistan or any other declared theocracy, but in the USA, nestled snugly away in a sparsely populated corner of the secular but devout republic. The Church of Jesus Christ of Latter Day Saints, or Mormons, are conservative and patriarchal enough, and the breakaway splinter groups who call themselves Fundamentalist Latter Day Saints are even more so. The Mormon Church, under pressure, adapted to modernity just slightly at the end of the nineteenth century by repudiating polygamy, while the FLDS just said no to modernity by refusing to repudiate polygamy. To Mormons now, both polygamy and the FLDS are something of an embarrassment. To the FLDS, Mormons are just part of 'the world', and that's not a compliment.

During the Depression a group of men founded the FLDS and settled in Short Creek (now called Colorado City), Arizona. The polygamist group was not popular with neighbours, because the multiple wives were on welfare and the abundant children attended state schools but the FLDS adults did not pay taxes. Arizona governor Howard Pyle hired private detectives to investigate Short Creek, and on 26 July 1953 Pyle ordered a massive police raid. He said, 'Here is a community ...dedicated to the wicked theory that every maturing girl child should be forced into the bondage of multiple wifehood with men of all ages for the sole purpose of producing more children to be reared to become mere chattels.'[14] Newsreels showed children in pyjamas yanked away from parents in the pre-dawn raid; the resulting public relations disaster caused Pyle to lose his bid for re-election. Officials were reluctant to take any further action against polygamist groups for decades. It was during this period that Carolyn Jessop, like many other girls, was abruptly married to a stranger when she was 18 (see page 19).

In 2003 members of the FLDS living in Colorado City began relocating to a 1,700-acre compound in Eldorado, Texas in order to escape renewed police scrutiny. The compound was surrounded by a fence and the gates were guarded; behind those gates the FLDS hoped to practise their religion in secrecy.[15] In May 2006 the FLDS leader Warren Jeffs was placed on the FBI's 'Ten Most Wanted' list for 'unlawful flight to avoid prosecution – sexual conduct with a minor, conspiracy to commit sexual conduct with a minor'.[16] He went on trial in September 2007 and was convicted in less than a month.

The chief witness for the prosecution was Elissa Wall, who was 'Jane Doe' during the trial but went public after it was over. She said on the stand that as a young girl she was taught there was a high price for disobeying religious leaders: the loss of heaven and salvation. Warren Jeffs was the prophet, and the prophet was a God to them, 'a God on earth'.

> 'We were to follow them obediently as though we were led by a hair,' she said, a hair that if snapped would cause them to 'forfeit our chance at an afterlife.'[17]

The following May, after the raid on the Yearning for Zion ranch, Wall talked about what this obedience had felt like:

> 'I was trapped,' recalled Wall, who is now in her early 20s. 'I felt like I had nowhere to turn. I so bad did not want to go through with marriage. I felt honestly what it was like to die.
>
> 'I remember thinking "if there's somewhere to run, I would." But there wasn't. There was nowhere to go. And I had to cross this threshold, and that was the day that truly changed my life,' she said.[18]

During the trial *The Salt Lake Tribune* published the transcript of a lesson Warren Jeffs gave to an Alta Academy home economics class in 1998, the year the school closed. Alta Academy was an FLDS school located inside the Jeffs family compound, where Warren Jeffs was the principal for 22 years, and in that role he 'set about making students live up to this motto: Perfect obedience produces perfect faith, which produces perfect people'.[19] His lectures were taped, and many FLDS members used the tapes as child-rearing tools; a much-repeated theme was the need to follow a single, God-anointed male leader. 'That one man is as God over the people and has the right to rule in all areas of life.'[20]

The 1998 lecture was titled 'Specific Duties and Counsel to the Mothers: How to Become One with Your Priesthood Head; A Woman Never Has the Right to Correct A Sister-Wife'. Jeffs tells the girls he wants to bring to their minds the real purposes of life and of priesthood marriage. God has put us in the world to meet two opposite powers, and the right way is Priesthood. 'If Priesthood is not involved in something, we should not want it.' The Priesthood is a form of power which God places into a man. Women do not have 'the holy Priesthood' but they have the power of it through their husbands, or their fathers if they are not married. When a woman is 'sealed to' a man, she becomes part of him. Not all of him, Jeffs emphasized; part of him. 'The woman who wants to be everything, will seek to rule over her husband.' In the world today men and women battle over their rights, so Jeffs reminds them of what the Prophet said: it takes a man and many women to make a man. He didn't say what it takes to make a woman, so one is left to assume that that takes only a fraction of a man, or perhaps just a little chemistry. At any rate the only real way to be a woman and fulfil one's calling as a woman is to 'be in oneness with the Priesthood bearer you will become part of'.

Until then, girls are taught (as Jeffs is teaching them in saying all this) to 'resist every temptation', to 'withdraw from every male with an improper connection'.

> When you enter into the Celestial Law, you will still keep all those bars up, all that resistance to all male people except the one man you are given to.[21]

The one man you are given to – that's how taken for granted it is, that women or girls are simply *given* like parcels. There is no question of choice or liking or compatibility, and no opportunity for it either, since the sexes are kept rigorously separate. The arrangement is: complete isolation from men and boys until puberty, and then being 'given' to one – unknown – man, and that man you are required to think of as a god. But what if in fact he is merely an ordinary human being, but one who has been raised to think he is your absolute superior, that he has the Priesthood and you don't, and in fact you don't like him or respect him and he doesn't treat you well? What then?

Then nothing. It's your problem.

> You give your will, you confide in him, your all centers in him.
>
> You wake up each day yearning to please him. You rejoice in his will towards you. You pray for him, you seek his counsel … His first loyalty is to Priesthood and to the Prophet. And because he loves God and the Prophet, he is able to love you and lead you right.[22]

That's it. That's the safeguard. That's how they can be so confident that it will be unproblematic to 'give' a teenage girl to an unknown man who has complete authority over her and whom she is ordered to obey and more or less worship. That's the safeguard, that's the answer to the question 'but what if he's selfish and demanding and unkind and a bully?' Because he loves God and the Prophet, he won't be those things, or if he is, those are the right things for him to be. In other words reality is beside the point, actions and behaviour are beside the point, personal qualities are beside the point. The *point* is simply the rule, the formula, the algorithm: because he loves God and the Prophet he is able to love you and lead you right. It's like a recipe, or arithmetic. Add milk to egg yolks and you get custard, add two to three and you get five. Add loves God and the Prophet to a male human being and you get rightness.

Jeffs reminds the students again that the husband 'shall rule over' the woman, and he cites Brigham Young saying that to 'perfect their lives' women must completely submit. But – they must do it willingly. They must live an oxymoron.

> And so you ladies, to fulfill that command of the great Jehovah that, 'Your desires shall be to your husband and he shall rule over you,' it requires you willingly submit.[23]

It *requires* you *willingly submit* – it requires you square the circle. If the submission is required, then it's not in the normal sense willing; but Jeffs' method of persuasion has more to do with repetition than with logic.

It's impossible not to notice what a very convenient theology this is, for the men who originated it and the ones who perpetuate and preach and enforce it. It's impossible not to think that 'God and the Prophet' are simply a fig leaf for a naked and brazen system of sexual slavery. It's impossible not to think of the fortunate men of the FLDS (not all FLDS men are fortunate in this sense, to put it mildly – many adolescent boys are summarily expelled from the community for various trivial offences, which takes care of the problem of surplus men which polygamy naturally creates) as a group of stags or silverbacks cornering and bossing a group of females for sexual purposes. It is impossible not to realize that this religion puts a glow of sanctity on an arrangement in which older men get to have exclusive sex with a variety of young women and girls, with no arguments, no resistance, no back talk. Matt Ridley could have been (but wasn't) describing the FLDS when he wrote in *The Red Queen* (1993):

> The harems of ancient despots revealed that men are capable of making the most of opportunities to turn rank into reproductive success, but they cannot have been typical of the human condition for most of its history. About the only way to be a harem-guarding potentate nowadays is to start a cult and brainwash potential concubines about your holiness.[24]

When in doubt, slice the genitals off

Perhaps the FLDS women and girls can count themselves lucky, though: they at least aren't mutilated. Control of their genitals is exercised through control of their entire bodies, and their minds, rather than through slicing off and sewing closed the genitalia themselves. In parts of Africa that is what does happen.

There are many African women who campaign against female genital mutilation. One is Nahid Toubia, the first woman surgeon in Sudan, who served as the head of the Paediatric Surgery department at Khartoum teaching hospital for many years and is now an Assistant Professor at Columbia University School of Public Health and a director of Human Rights Watch.

Another is Waris Dirie, a model from Somalia who has been campaigning against FGM since 1996. When Dirie was 5 years old, her mother held her down on a rock while another woman cut off parts of her genitals with a razor blade and sewed up what was left with coarse thread. There was no anaesthetic, and the wound later became infected.

> The agony she suffered was in part what spurred her to leave the Somali desert community she had grown up in, and escape to London …Waris says what she went through will never leave her.
>
> 'Every day I still struggle to understand why this has happened to me – this cruel and terrible thing for which there is no reason or explanation – whatever they tell you about religion or purity. I can't tell you how angry I feel, how furious it makes me.'[25]

There are feminists and NGOs in the rest of the world campaigning against FGM, along with UN organizations such as the WHO, UNICEF and UNFPA. There are also opponents and critics of these campaigns, not only in the places where FGM is traditional (but the opponents of the campaigns don't call it 'mutilation', of course, preferring 'cutting' or 'circumcision' or 'surgery' or 'reshaping'), but also among academics of a left or progressive bent, just the people one would expect to be opposed to customary practices which harm women – until one remembers that concerns about cultural imperialism trump women's rights.

One such critic is Richard Shweder, a cultural anthropologist at the University of Chicago, whose 2003 paper 'When Cultures Collide: Which Rights? Whose Tradition of Values?' is sharply critical of what he calls 'a flawed game whose rules have been fixed by the rich nations of the world' and an example of 'cultural globalization'.

Shweder begins by citing concern at 'the highly visible global campaign' against a commonplace East and West African 'cultural practice', one which is 'socially endorsed and highly valued by many ethnic groups in nations such as Mali, Sierra Leone, the Gambia, Egypt, Ethiopia, Somalia, the Sudan and Kenya'. That claim is central to his concern at the highly visible global campaign: it is the familiar (and often reasonable) anti-colonialist anti-imperialist worry about outsiders meddling with the valued traditions and practices of relatively powerless others. But it is also a flawed claim, because it makes a common but nonetheless drastic mistake: it claims that the practice (of 'surgical modification' of genitals, as he characterizes it) is highly valued by many ethnic groups.

But literally speaking, groups don't value things. Groups can't literally value anything, any more than nations or communities or families can, because groups don't have minds. It is only people (and some animals) who can value cultural practices, because it is only people who have minds, and they have them in the singular, one at a time. Their thoughts can't ever be added together to make a larger, group thought, which then becomes 'what the group thinks'. Thoughts can't be poured into a large bowl to make soup; they can only be added to a pile of distinct entities, with the entities remaining distinct. The thoughts of different people never melt into each other, no matter how high the heat.

Of course it makes sense and it is idiomatic to say that groups think this and value that, and sociologists necessarily talk about groups in abstract terms in order to analyse broad social phenomena, but the difficulty is that however idiomatic and sociologically sensible the usage is it can obscure the reality that groups don't *literally* value anything.

Martha Nussbaum put the idea this way in *The Feminist Critique of Liberalism*, addressing the question of what it means to make the individual the basic unit for political thought:

> It means, first of all, that liberalism responds sharply to the basic fact that each individual has a course from birth to death that is not precisely the same as that of any other person; that each person is one and not more than one, that each feels pain in his or her own body, that the food given to A does not arrive in the stomach of B. The separateness of persons is a basic fact of human life; in stressing it, liberalism stresses something experientially true and fundamentally important ... It says that the fundamental entity for politics is a living body that goes from here to there, from birth to death, never fused with any other – that we are hungry and joyful and loving and needy one by one, however closely we may embrace one another. In normative terms, this commitment to the recognition of individual separateness means, for the liberal, that the demands of a collectivity or a relation should not as such be made the basic goal of politics: collectivities, such as the state and even the family, are composed of individuals, who never do fuse, who always continue to have their separate brains and voices and stomachs, however much they love each other.[26]

One can always take polls, of course, and add up the numbers of people who say 'approve' and those who say 'disapprove' on any given question, and then conclude that 27 per cent or 54 per cent or 79 per cent approve of whatever it may be. But that is usually a radical simplification, which boils down a range of attitudes and degrees of intensity into a yes or no, and in any case that is still not the same thing as saying the group (or even a particular percentage of the group) thinks X, because it is still a collection of separate people each thinking (or claiming to think) X.

Well, of course, that's what Shweder means, one might say: he means that the people in the group value the practice. Yes, but the trouble with that is, he doesn't know that all the people in the group value the practice, and in fact that question is very important. There is very good evidence that many children do not value the practice while it is being done to them and during the long painful healing process afterwards; there is also good evidence that many parents don't value it and would prefer not to inflict it on their children, but bow to social pressure. Saying that the practice is highly valued by groups covertly decides one of the very issues being contested, by claiming a unanimity that is not known to exist and often is known not to exist.

This is all the more noteworthy because much of what Shweder objects to is precisely uniformity, of practice and of opinion, yet he himself verbally imposes uniformity of opinion on the very ethnic groups he would seek to protect from the uniformity of 'cultural globalization'.[27]

This is the paradox that multiculturalism always bumps up against, of course, as is becoming increasingly well known. Multiculturalism by definition makes a fetish of cultures, and it is almost impossible to do that without treating them as monolithic. As soon as you admit that all cultures have internal dissent and disagreement and nonconformity, the whole idea of protecting or deferring to particular 'cultures' breaks down into incoherence, as Kenan Malik argues.

> The logic of the preservationist argument is that every culture has a pristine form, its original state. It decays when it is no longer in that form. Like racial scientists with their idea of racial type, some modern multiculturalists appear to hold a belief in cultural type. For racial scientists, a 'type' was a group of human beings linked by a set of fundamental characteristics which were unique to it. Each type was separated from others by a sharp discontinuity; there was rarely any doubt as to which type an individual belonged. Each type remained constant through time. There were severe limits to how much any member of a type could drift away from the fundamental ground plan by which the type was constituted. These, of course, are the very

characteristics that constitute a culture in much of today's multiculturalism talk. Many multiculturalists, like racial scientists, have come
to think of human types as fixed, unchanging entities, each defined by its
special essence.[28]

There was some public discussion of the issue in November and
December 2007 when *The New York Times* science columnist John
Tierney noted that the American Anthropological Association's
annual meeting would be debating whether critics of FGM are
'guilty of ignorance and cultural imperialism'. He quoted the AAA:

> The panel includes for the first time, the critical 'third wave' or
> multicultural feminist perspectives of circumcised African women scholars
> Wairimu Njambi, a Kenyan, and Fuambai Ahmadu, a Sierra Leonean. Both
> women hail from cultures where female and male initiation rituals are the
> norm and have written about their largely positive and contextualized
> experiences, creating an emergent discursive space for a hitherto 'muted
> group' in global debates about FGC.[29]

This is an interesting idea, because when it comes to physical reality
the 'muted group' would seem to be not African scholars who
support FGM but very young girls being held forcibly down while
their genitals are cut off. In places where FGM is the cultural norm,
supporters of FGM are of course not a muted group at all; they are
the group that prevails while the weaker, muted group is that of the
girls and also of parents who would prefer not to cut their daughters.
The AAA's concern for muted groups seems slightly selective – but
that is a vocational hazard of anthropology: anthropologists are
interested in cultures as such, so there is a natural pull towards
preservationism with respect to any particular culture. The rest of us
can agree that knowledge of cultures is highly valuable while still
thinking that actually cruel and damaging practices should be done
away with.

The rest of us can, but not all the rest of us do. There was a sharp
disagreement between what the AAA calls the critical third wave
multiculturalist feminist perspective and perspectives of various other

kinds on the Women's Studies email list in January 2008. It started when two or three people (including one of us) expressed strong surprise that the practice was being referred to as circumcision when we'd have thought it was well known – at least to people in Women's Studies – that that word was considered both euphemistic and drastically inaccurate, since most FGM removes a great deal more than the equivalent of the foreskin. A heated discussion ensued.

One participant cited a book titled *Genital Cutting and Transnational Sisterhood: Disputing US Polemics*, thus hinting that 'US polemics' need to be disputed more than genital cutting does; this seems an odd take for someone in Women's Studies.

> This collection of essays problematizes the 'M' for mutilation (which I thought was a critique by now well-entrenched in Women's Studies) …The book does a very nice job of pointing out that while no one is turning cartwheels about female genital surgeries, and that African women themselves have taken steps to end such practices, this is a far cry from the explicitly colonialist and ethnocentric outrage voiced by Western feminists about practices in 'other' countries, as performed precisely on cue on this listserv, according to a script that seems not to have changed in 20 years.

The problem here is that, not surprisingly, there *was* no 'explicitly colonialist and ethnocentric outrage'. It would have been very odd if there had been. What, on a notoriously multiculturally correct (to coin a phrase) mailing list, talk in terms of explicitly colonialist and ethnocentric outrage? It's hard even to imagine what that would look like. No, there was no such; there was only explicit rejection of this particular practice, which is also passionately rejected by many African women themselves on perfectly reasonable and universalizable grounds: they remember the agony of the procedure and they don't like what it did to their bodies.

Ayaan Hirsi Ali joins Waris Dirie in describing that experience. Her grandmother (who had the cutting done while Hirsi Ali's father was a political prisoner and her mother was away, against their known wishes) held her upper body and two other women held her legs apart.

> Then the scissors went down between my legs and the man cut off my
> inner labia and my clitoris. I heard it, like a butcher snipping the fat off
> a piece of meat. A piercing pain shot up between my legs,
> indescribable, and I howled. Then came the sewing: the long, blunt
> needle clumsily pushed into my bleeding outer labia, my loud and
> anguished protests …[30]

That's not explicitly colonialist and ethnocentric outrage, it's just outrage.

Punishment

As we write, a story appears in the *Observer* of a man in Basra who stamped on, suffocated and then stabbed to death his 17-year-old daughter for becoming infatuated with a British soldier. He was arrested but released after two hours, and he told the two *Observer* reporters that the police congratulated him for what he had done. 'They are men and know what honour is,' he said.

Rand Abdel-Qader was studying English at Basra University; she met the British soldier, 'Paul', when she worked as a volunteer helping displaced families. Their relationship apparently amounted to a few conversations over four months, but her father learned she had been seen in public talking to Paul. Her mother called Rand's two brothers to stop Abdel-Qader Ali as he choked her with his foot on her throat, but instead they joined in. They then threw her body into a makeshift grave while her uncles spat on it. The *Observer* reporters talked to him in the garden of his home two weeks later, and found him proud of what he'd done. His only regret, he told them, was that he hadn't killed his daughter at birth. 'If I had realised then what she would become, I would have killed her the instant her mother delivered her,' he explained.

'Death was the least she deserved,' said Abdel-Qader. 'I don't regret it. I had the support of all my friends who are fathers, like me, and know what she did was unacceptable to any Muslim that honours his religion,' he said.

Abdel-Qader says his daughter's 'bad genes' were passed on from her mother. That mother went into hiding after divorcing her husband after the killing; she was afraid of retribution from his family. She was scarred from the beating he gave her, in which he broke her arm. She went to a cousin's house when she left but notes were delivered to the door every day saying she was a prostitute and deserved the same death as Rand.

'She was killed by animals. Every night when I go to bed I remember the face of Rand calling for help while her father and brothers ended her life,' she said, tears streaming down her face.

Abdel-Qader Ali, however, is cheerful.

'I don't have a daughter now, and I prefer to say that I never had one. That girl humiliated me in front of my family and friends ...Our girls should respect their religion, their family and their bodies.

'I have only two boys from now on. That girl was a mistake in my life. I know God is blessing me for what I did,' he said, his voice swelling with pride. 'My sons are by my side, and they were men enough to help me finish the life of someone who just brought shame to ours.'[31]

That was 11 May. On 1 June a follow-up story appeared: the conclusion to the story of Rand's mother, Leila Hussein: the story of what happened after the divorce, the broken arm, the fear and hiding, the notes calling her a prostitute and saying she deserved death, the memories of Rand calling for help while her father and brothers killed her, the tears. Five weeks after she told the *Observer* the story of Rand's murder – five weeks when she lived in fear – Leila Hussein was murdered.

Afif Sarhan and Caroline Davies reported in the *Observer* that Leila lived her last few weeks in terror, moving from safe house to safe house and staying no more than four days in each. She thought she would soon be safe: arrangements were under way to smuggle her to Amman, and she was on her way to meet the person who was going to help her escape when a car stopped beside her and the two women who were walking her to a taxi. Five bullets were fired; three of them hit Leila, and she died in hospital despite efforts to save her.

Leila had put herself in danger by leaving her husband, as she told the *Observer* in April.

> 'No man can accept being left by a woman in Iraq. But I would prefer to be killed than sleep in the same bed as a man who was able to do what he did to his own daughter.'[32]

Leila went to a small women's rights organization in Basra, and that's when the threats began. She had been staying at the house of one of the women's rights campaigners, 'Mariam' (a pseudonym), and it was from there that the two of them and another campaigner, 'Faisal', left to meet the contact who would take Leila to Jordan.

> 'Leila was anxious, but she was also happy at having the chance to leave Iraq,' said Mariam ... 'She had not been able to sleep the night before. I stayed up talking to her about her plans after she arrived in Amman. I gave her some clothes to take with her and she was packing the only bag she had. She was too excited to sleep.'
>
> Mariam said that when she awoke Leila had already prepared breakfast, cleaned her house and even baked a date cake as a thank-you for the help she had been given.[33]

All three of them were shot, and as Mariam lay in her hospital bed she could hear people talking about Leila's murder in the corridor.

> 'I could hear people talking on the corridors and the only thing that they had to say was that Leila was wrong for defending her daughter's mistakes and that her death was God's punishment.'[34]

It's an ugly business, men who love a religion and a putative deity and hate women enough to murder them, even (or rather especially) when they are their own wives, daughters, sisters, mothers. The unknown unseen God is everything and the living breathing daughter and mother are nothing, or are enemies who deserve death.

5 Holy Groupthink

In July 2008 an 'interfaith conference' took place in Madrid, convened by King Abdullah of Saudi Arabia and paid for by the Muslim World League, a Wahhabist NGO funded largely by the Saudis. The conference's stated aim was to call for 'constructive dialogue among followers of religions'.

In his opening address King Abdullah said:

> Mankind is suffering today from a loss of values and conceptual confusion, and is passing through a critical phase which, in spite of all the scientific progress, is witnessing a proliferation of crime, an increase in terrorism, the disintegration of the family, subversion of the minds of the young by drug-abuse, exploitation of the poor by the strong, and odious racist tendencies. This is all a consequence of the spiritual void from which people suffer when they forget God ... There is no solution for us other than to agree on a united approach, through dialogue among religions and civilizations.[1]

People are suffering from a spiritual void because they have forgotten God, and as a result there is 1) more crime; 2) more terrorism; 3) disintegration of the family; 4) damage to young minds from drug abuse; 5) exploitation of the poor; and 6) racism. On 1), crime rates have declined in many places in the past four decades. On 2), it hardly needs pointing out that most contemporary terrorism is in fact inspired by the remembrance of God. We'll return to 3) in a moment. On 4), Iran has one of the highest rates of drug use in the region.[2] In Afghanistan, the Taliban made $300 million from the opium trade in 2007, according to UN estimates; this year they have cut back on poppy cultivation in an effort to keep prices high.[3] On 5) and 6), it is true that there is exploitation of the poor and that there is racism, but there is not much evidence that people who remember God do better on that score than people who forget God. On the contrary, King Abdullah's own god-remembering Saudi Arabia is notorious for widespread abuse of domestic servants from places like the Philippines, Indonesia and Bangladesh. Human Rights Watch released a report on 'Abuses against Asian Domestic Workers in Saudi Arabia' only a week before the king's address.

> Approximately 1.5 million women domestic workers, primarily from Indonesia, Sri Lanka, and the Philippines, work in Saudi Arabia ...While many domestic workers enjoy decent work conditions, others endure a range of abuses including non-payment of salaries, forced confinement, food deprivation, excessive workload, and instances of severe psychological, physical, and sexual abuse. Human Rights Watch documented dozens of cases where the combination of these conditions amounted to forced labor, trafficking, or slavery-like conditions.[4]

Moreover, the king makes no mention of oppression of or violence against women. (Most domestic servants in Saudi Arabia are women. They are poor, of 'other' races, and women, so potentially triply subject to abuse.) There is no mention of women, period. Instead there is mention of 'the disintegration of the family'. What does that mean? In the mouth of the Saudi king as in the mouths of other religious fundamentalists, it generally means that ideas of what the family can and should be, especially ideas about the rights and responsibilities of women in the family, have changed in ways that the pious don't like.

The king's basic claim, that forgetting God causes that particular list of problems, seems to have no merit – but the genre it belongs to is a hardy perennial: everything is going badly; repent and return to God.

The king was invoking not just propositional beliefs but also group or community loyalty. That is one of the jobs that religions do: they provide followers with a sense of community. That fact is one of the complications in discussing and especially in criticizing religion: religion is a set of truth claims, but it is other things too, and the other things are highly valued and so tend to shield the truth claims from criticism and honest discussion. This means the truth claims go on perpetuating themselves, and efforts to find better sources of the other things are weakened or blocked.

As anthropologists and sociologists have pointed out, a sense of community is high on the list of other things that religion offers – so high that religion attracts many people who don't actually believe any of the truth claims. A big part of the pull of the mosque or church or temple has to do with the rewards of belonging to a social group and the attendant feelings of loyalty, solidarity, belonging, unity, protection, continuity over time, and the like. 'The *ummah*' has a nice sound to it for its members – but for non-members it can function more as a reminder of hostility to outsiders: always the paradox of community.

Solidarity is a powerful drive, but it is also a decidedly equivocal gift. Its very power makes it dangerous, in the tendency to unite against non-members[5] and in the practice of enforcing obedience and conformity on members. Community and community feeling can motivate people to set aside normal canons of epistemology in favour of loyalty to the community and what it believes. A community, of course, can't actually believe anything, only the members can, but that's just why group loyalty puts so much pressure on members to believe what others believe: so that it can *seem* that the community itself does believe. If conformity is 100 per cent, it becomes in a sense accurate to say that 'the community believes', and people often have a strong desire to be able to say that.

The result is a displacement of the actually reliable ways of testing truth claims, and the substitution of thoroughly unreliable ones. If the truth claims are trivial enough, this may not matter much, but religious truth claims are by no means always and reliably trivial. As we have seen, they often declare some kinds of people subordinate to other kinds of people, and they also often deny the right of humans to contradict such claims.

At a meeting of the UN Human Rights Council on 16 June 2008, David Littman, NGO Representative of the Association for World Education, was given the floor to deliver a joint statement for the AWE and the International Humanist and Ethical Union under agenda item Eight: Integrating the Human Rights of Women throughout the United Nations system. Twenty-two seconds after he began, he was stopped by the delegate of Egypt, Amr Roshdy Hassan. The delegate, according to Littman and to Roy Brown of the IHEU, had broken protocol by arranging to receive advance copies of the AWE and IHEU statements. When Hassan stopped Littman he said, 'The first paragraph, you talk about Egypt and the Sharia law. In the second paragraph you talk about Sudan, Pakistan and the Sharia law. The third and fourth paragraphs are on the Sharia law.' In fact Littman hadn't mentioned Sharia when he was interrupted.

Pakistan then joined Egypt.

> We have strong objections on any discussion, any direct or indirect discussion, any out of context, selective discussion on the Sharia law in this Council.

Then Egypt became more heated.

> What we are talking now about is not about the right of NGOs to speak but about the Sharia law and whether it is admissible to discuss it in this Council. I appeal to my colleague from Slovenia not to accept any discussion of the Sharia law in this Council because it will not happen. And we will not take this lightly.

Pakistan joined in again.

> I would like to state again that this is not the forum to discuss religious sensitivity. It will amount to spreading hatred against certain members of the Council.

After further exchanges the President of the HRC called for a break; 40 minutes later the meeting resumed and the president warned Littman against 'making a judgement or evaluation of any particular set of legislation' and allowed him to continue. Littman quoted from the Report by the Special Rapporteur Halima Warzazi on Female Genital Mutilation, and Egypt stopped him again.

> This is an attempt to raise a bad traditional practice to Islam …My last part, Sir, is that is regardless of the result of the vote, I couldn't care less if I will win or lose this vote. My point is that Islam will not be crucified in this Council.[6]

'My point is that Islam will not be crucified in this Council.' Hassan seems to have spoken with much passion – as one might say 'Give me liberty or give me death' or 'I have seen the Promised Land' or 'Free at last, free at last, thank God almighty we are free at last'. But what is the passion about? It's about protecting an abstraction, a particular religion, which itself has no mind or body with which to experience protection or freedom or criticism or anything else, from the comments of someone seeking to promote the freedom and rights of *actual living feeling* human beings.

The passion of 'give me liberty' or 'free at last' is about real freedom for real people; the passion of 'Islam will not be crucified' is about specious protection for a social construct at the expense of real people.

This is how group feeling and community and solidarity operate to crush individual aspirations and freedoms and rights. The value of the community is placed above all other value, then any perceived insult or offence to the community is interpreted as a deep psychic wound to all the members of the community, and the result is that the values, rules and standards of the community are made sacrosanct and entirely beyond criticism and reform. This naturally means that the most powerful members of the community get to determine the rules to which all the members must conform.

To some extent, of course, this arrangement is in place

everywhere. There is always some bias in favour of the status quo, of how we do things around here, of acting normally. But in open societies there is also, competing with that, an acceptance of and familiarity with the benefits of change, reform, progress, improvement, and the free discussion and criticism that make improvement possible. Engineers don't cry out that 'the blueprint will not be crucified' if someone suggests a possible improvement.

Campaigning against human rights

David Littman reported in a 1999 article on 'Universal human rights and "human rights in Islam" ' that certain member states of the United Nations have been making a systematic effort to replace 'some of the dominant paradigms of international relations', especially with respect to human rights.

> For example, representatives of the Islamic Republic of Iran continue – in all fora – to press their objections to the universal character and indivisibility of human rights, as interpreted in the Universal Declaration of Human Rights (UDHR), which according to them, is a Western secular concept of Judeo-Christian origin, incompatible with the sacred Islamic *shari'a*.[7]

In 1981 Iran's representative at the UN stated at the thirty-sixth UN General Assembly session 'that the UDHR represented a secular interpretation of the Judeo-Christian tradition which could not be implemented by Muslims; if a choice had to be made between its stipulations and "the divine law of the country," Iran would always choose Islamic law'.[8] Also in 1981 the Universal Islamic Declaration of Human Rights (UIDHR) was presented to UNESCO in Paris. It was prepared under the auspices of the Islamic Council, a London-based organization affiliated with the Muslim World League.

In 1984 the Iranian representative told the UN General Assembly what his country thought of the UDHR.

Man was of divine origin and human dignity could not be reduced to a series of secular norms ... certain concepts contained in the Universal Declaration of Human Rights needed to be revised. [Iran] recognized no authority or power but that of Almighty God and no legal tradition apart from Islamic law ... conventions, declarations and resolutions or decisions of international organizations which were contrary to Islam had no validity in the Islamic Republic of Iran ... The Universal Declaration of Human Rights, which represented a secular understanding of the Judeo-Christian tradition, could not be implemented by Muslims and did not accord with the system of values recognized by the Islamic Republic of Iran; his country would therefore not hesitate to violate its provisions, since it had to choose between violating the divine law of the country and violating secular conventions.[9]

In 1990 the Cairo Declaration on Human Rights in Islam was adopted by the nineteenth Islamic Conference of Foreign Ministers of the Organisation of the Islamic Conference. The CDHRI establishes Sharia as 'the only source of reference' for the protection of human rights in Islamic countries, thus giving it supremacy over the UDHR.

In 1992 Iranian Ambassador Sirous Nasseri told the Human Rights Committee:

many peoples were not satisfied with the rigid application of human rights instruments and wanted account taken of their traditions, culture and religious context in order to evaluate the human rights situation in a country ... The Islamic countries had therefore elaborated an Islamic Declaration of Human Rights.[10]

In March 1998 Iranian Foreign Minister Dr Kamal Kharazi spoke at the Jubilee Commemoration of the UDHR at the Commission on Human Rights in Geneva. His statement contained an appeal for revision of the UDHR along with a request that the High Commissioner 'invite commentaries on the UDHR as a prelude to dialogue'.[11]

Which rights?

The Universal Declaration of Human Rights (UDHR) begins with a preamble, the first clause of which says

> Whereas recognition of the inherent dignity and of the equal and inalienable rights of all members of the human family is the foundation of freedom, justice and peace in the world ...[12]

The Cairo Declaration on Human Rights in Islam (CDHRI) also begins with a preamble; its first clause is quite different:

> Reaffirming the civilizing and historical role of the Islamic Ummah which God made the best nation that has given mankind a universal and well-balanced civilization in which harmony is established between this life and the hereafter and knowledge is combined with faith; and the role that this Ummah should play to guide a humanity confused by competing trends and ideologies and to provide solutions to the chronic problems of this materialistic civilization ...[13]

We are in different worlds already. The UDHR, because it is *universal* and because the universality is the whole point, does not carve up the human family into nations or religions, while the CDHRI does exactly that from the very beginning. The UDHR starts with the rights of all human beings; the CDHRI starts with the superiority of the Islamic *ummah*. In short the CDHRI subverts the entire purpose of the UDHR in its very first words.

The UDHR preamble's second clause makes clear why the universality and equality of rights are so important and why the invocation of the superiority of a particular community is so sharply – so pointedly, even wickedly – at odds with the purpose of the UDHR.

> Whereas disregard and contempt for human rights have resulted in barbarous acts which have outraged the conscience of mankind ...[14]

The Universal Declaration of Human Rights was drawn up in the aftermath of World War II and its attendant horrors: the Nazi genocide; the near-genocidal forced labour on the Burma railway, in which more than 80,000 out of 200,000 slave labourers died as well as an estimated 16,000 prisoners of war;[15] the bombings of Dresden, Tokyo, Hiroshima and Nagasaki; the immense death toll in the Soviet Union, which wiped out 10 per cent of the population.[16] The human rights in question had to be universal in order to address 'barbarous acts which have outraged the conscience of mankind'; if the human rights are particular then we're right back where we started, committing barbarous acts against people who are not members of 'the best nation'. As with the CDHRI we're right back where we started.

Article 1 of the UDHR is brief and to the point.

> All human beings are born free and equal in dignity and rights. They are endowed with reason and conscience and should act towards one another in a spirit of brotherhood.[17]

Article 1 of the CDHRI is longer and of very different import.

(a)   All human beings form one family whose members are united by submission to God and descent from Adam. All men are equal in terms of basic human dignity and basic obligations and responsibilities, without any discrimination on the grounds of race, colour, language, sex, religious belief, political affiliation, social status or other considerations. True faith is the guarantee for enhancing such dignity along the path to human perfection.

(b)   All human beings are God's subjects, and the most loved by Him are those who are most useful to the rest of His subjects, and no one has superiority over another except on the basis of piety and good deeds.[18]

The first sentence makes membership in the human family dependent on submission to God, which the UDHR refrains from doing; the CDHRI thus effectively narrows the application of a declaration of rights which is supposed of its very essence to apply to all human beings without exception. Where the UD says 'all human beings' the CD says 'all men'. The UD cites universal reason and conscience while the CD not only mentions 'true faith' (which must exclude people who have 'false faith'), it also makes 'true faith' the guarantee of human dignity. In the UD rights and dignity are inherent rather than conditional, while in the CD they are conditional rather than inherent. Clause (b) divides human beings further by specifying which ones are most loved by God. It asserts the concept of superiority of some human beings over other human beings, which is deliberately and necessarily absent from the UD.

Article 2 of the UDHR declares everyone entitled to all the stipulated rights and freedoms 'without distinction of any kind'. Article 2 of the CDHRI makes rights conditional on Sharia:

(a)   Life is a God-given gift and the right to life is guaranteed to every human being. It is the duty of individuals, societies and state to protect this right from any violation, and it is prohibited to take away life except for a Shari'a prescribed reason ...

(d)   Safety from bodily harm is a guaranteed right. It is the duty of the state to safeguard it, and it is prohibited to breach it without a Shari'a-prescribed reason.[19]

'Except for a Shari'a prescribed reason' simply negates the prohibition and renders it worthless; 'without a Shari'a-prescribed reason' of course does the same thing. There is something half-rude, half-frivolous about pretending to specify and guarantee a right only to snatch it away again by invoking religious law.

Article 5 of the UDHR says 'No one shall be subjected to torture or to cruel, inhuman or degrading treatment or punishment.' There is no matching article in the CDHRI; Article 19 (d) of the CD says 'There shall be no crime or punishment except as provided for in the Shari'a.' This, as the newspapers daily tell us, in many places is taken to include stoning to death, death for apostasy, amputation, 'honour' killings, death for homosexuality, whippings, and the like.

Article 16 of the UDHR declares rights of marriage.

(1)   Men and women of full age, without any limitation due to race, nationality or religion, have the right to marry and to found a

family. They are entitled to equal rights as to marriage, during marriage and at its dissolution.

(2)   Marriage shall be entered into only with the free and full consent of the intending spouses.[20]

Article 5 of the CDHRI does it differently.

(a)   The family is the foundation of society, and marriage is the basis of its formation. Men and women have the right to marriage, and no restrictions stemming from race, colour or nationality shall prevent them from enjoying this right.[21]

The CDHRI omits 'of full age' and also does not include religion among the forbidden restrictions; therefore, it would appear, restrictions stemming from religion *shall* prevent men and women (and men and girls) from enjoying this right. Sura 5.5 allows men to marry 'believers' and 'the virtuous women of those who received the Scripture before you'; it says nothing comparable to women. The CDHRI nowhere says that marriage shall be entered into only with the free and full consent of the intending spouses; therefore, it would appear, forced marriage is perfectly acceptable in the Cairo Declaration on Human Rights in Islam, and full consent is not seen as necessary therein.

The UDHR, as already noted, declares all human beings free and equal in the first Article and declares everyone entitled to all the stipulated rights and freedoms 'without distinction of any kind' in the second Article; it also says in the preamble that the peoples of the United Nations have reaffirmed their faith in the equal rights of men and women, so it has no need to specify rights for women again. The CDHRI says different things in its preamble and first two Articles, and in Article 6 it addresses the subject of women.

(a)   Woman is equal to man in human dignity, and has rights to enjoy as well as duties to perform; she has her own civil entity and financial independence, and the right to retain her name and lineage.

(b)   The husband is responsible for the support and welfare of the family.[22]

Article 6 does not say that women have equal rights with men, or that woman is equal to man in human rights; furthermore, by saying the husband is responsible for the support of the family, it removes responsibility and thus adult standing from women.

In Article 26 the UD declares a universal right to education, that parents have a right to choose, that education shall promote among other things 'understanding, tolerance and friendship among all nations, racial or religious groups'. The CDHRI takes a more parochial view in Article 7:

(a)   Parents and those in such like capacity have the right to choose the type of education they desire for their children, provided they take into consideration the interest and future of the children in accordance with ethical values and the principles of Shari'a.[23]

In Article 9 the CD declares:

The State shall ensure the availability of ways and means to acquire education and shall guarantee educational diversity in the interest of society so as to enable men to be acquainted with the religion of Islam and the facts of the Universe for the benefit of mankind.[24]

And that

(b)   Every human being has the right to receive both religious and worldly education from the various institution of, [sic] education and guidance, including the family, the school, the university, the media, etc., and in such an integrated and balanced manner as to develop his personality, strengthen his faith in God and promote his respect for and defence of both rights and obligations.[25]

There is no equivalent of any of this in the UD.

Article 10 of the CD, starkly, says

> Islam is the religion of unspoiled nature. It is prohibited to exercise any
> form of compulsion on man or to exploit his poverty or ignorance in order
> to convert him to another religion or to atheism.[26]

There is no right to leave 'the religion of unspoiled nature'. In many
majority-Muslim countries 'apostasy' – leaving Islam – is a capital
crime. There is, of course, nothing like this passage in the UD.

Article 11 of the CD repudiates colonialism in a way that the UD
does not, and this could be seen as a valuable expansion of the UD;
however, the first clause makes human beings subject to God, which
the UD also does not do.

> Human beings are born free, and no one has the right to enslave,
> humiliate, oppress or exploit them, and there can be no subjugation but
> to God the Most-High.[27]

In practice, since God the Most-High is not available, it is the human
representatives of God who do the subjugating, so the exception
again takes away what it seemed to give.

Article 12 of the CDHRI says

> Every man shall have the right, within the framework of Shari'a, to free
> movement and to select his place of residence whether inside or outside
> his country and if persecuted, is entitled to seek asylum in another
> country.[28]

It is well known that women in many majority-Muslim countries do
not have the right to free movement, and here the CD spells out that
lack of a right. This is one case where the generic 'he' really does
mean 'he' and not 'she' (which could indicate that other uses of
generic 'he' and 'man' in the CD also really mean 'he' and not 'she').

Article 19 of the CD says 'There shall be no crime or punishment
except as provided for in the Shari'a.' Since the crimes and
punishments provided for in the Shari'a are harsh enough, this
again is not a very valuable right.

Article 22 is positively alarming.

(a) Everyone shall have the right to express his opinion freely in such manner as would not be contrary to the principles of the Shari'a.

(b) Everyone shall have the right to advocate what is right, and propagate what is good, and warn against what is wrong and evil according to the norms of Islamic Shari'a.

(c) Information is a vital necessity to society. It may not be exploited or misused in such a way as may violate sanctities and the dignity of Prophets, undermine moral and ethical values or disintegrate, corrupt or harm society or weaken its faith.[29]

Article (c) essentially puts all efforts at reform at the mercy of clerical censors. A student and journalist in Afghanistan, Sayed Perwiz Kambakhsh, was sentenced to death for blasphemy in January 2008 for downloading an article from the internet about the treatment of women in Islam.[30]

Articles 24 and 25 make sure there is no mistake and no loophole.

Article 24

All the rights and freedoms stipulated in this Declaration are subject to the Islamic Shari'a.

Article 25

The Islamic Shari'a is the only source of reference for the explanation or classification of any of the articles of this Declaration.[31]

What's the difference?

The Cairo Declaration differs sharply from the Universal Declaration overall in its emphatic rejection of universalism, in rejecting the UD's 'without exception' in favour of firm, decided exceptions. In the detail, the CD differs from the UD in its avoidance of clarity, precision and openness and hence accountability and reliability. The Cairo Declaration injects exceptions into its concept of human rights, *without spelling out exactly what they entail*; this introduces a whole new element of doubt, uncertainty and fear into what is supposed to be a human rights document. Worse, it presents itself as a human rights document (of sorts) when in fact it puts anyone who subscribes to it in the position of (perhaps unknowingly) endorsing laws, restrictions and punishments that are human rights violations rather than human rights.

The *raison d'être* of the Cairo Declaration is the idea that the Universal Declaration is not in fact universal – that it is 'Western' and Judeo-Christian, that it does not work for non-Western cultures, that it 'could not be implemented by Muslims', in the words of the Iranian representative to the UN. So by comparing the two and finding how they differ it is possible to figure out what – in the view of the people who drew up the Cairo Declaration and those who signed on to it, at least – can be 'implemented by Muslims'.

We find out, generally, via Articles 24 and 25, that all rights are subject to Sharia, and via the Cairo Declaration as a whole, we find out that the authors are willing to make human rights subordinate to Sharia without ever spelling out what that could mean, what it presumably means, what in many countries governed by Sharia people take it to mean. The Cairo Declaration doesn't mention stoning to death for adultery, or the death penalty for apostasy, or forced marriage, or child marriage, or guardian laws, or laws forbidding women to travel, work, or go to school without male permission. The Cairo Declaration rejects the Universal Declaration, and stands out for its own version of human rights, yet it does it in a secretive way.

In fact it seems clear that the authors of the Cairo Declaration did not start with first principles and attempt to create the best human rights document they could, but rather that they started with existing regimes and legal codes in existing majority-Muslim countries, and then wrote the Cairo Declaration so that it would match the existing laws – adding 24 and 25 at the end in case they'd left anything out. This is bad enough, and the fact that this is done without transparency makes it even worse. The Cairo Declaration takes a declaration of rights that is, deliberately, as clear and open and explicit as possible, and renders it vague instead of precise, obscure instead of clear, tacit instead of explicit. It injects an element – a large element – of uncertainty and danger; in article after article, it merely invokes Sharia without saying what that means. With the Universal Declaration we know where we are and with the Cairo Declaration we don't – the rights are limited, and in ways that are not specified or spelled out. The Universal Declaration is *both* general *and* specific; the Cairo Declaration is particular where the Universal Declaration is general, and vague where the UD is precise.

The result is that the Cairo Declaration does away with the transparency, clarity and specificity, and hence the accountability and also the confidence necessary in a declaration of rights. The worst case scenario is that the CD's repeated refrain of 'except as permitted by Shari'a' means what it appears to mean: permitted by Sharia as in the laws of Saudi Arabia, Iran, Pakistan, Egypt, and so on. There is absolutely nothing in the CD to indicate that 'except as permitted by Sharia' would be in the smallest degree milder than its most brutal real-world instantiations.

The Cairo Declaration is an oddity, in a way, because it has no clear standing or authority. Its foundations are as cryptic and doubtful as all the 'except for a Shari'a prescribed reason' clauses – and for much the same reasons. Critics of Sharia are often reprovingly told that there is no such thing as Sharia in the sense of one, unified, universally agreed-on Sharia; that interpretations and applications differ, and it is Orientalist and essentialist to attempt to criticize this imaginary 'Sharia'. But if that's the case, what is Sharia doing in the Cairo Declaration? The authors of the CD seem to consider 'Sharia' understandable enough to cite as that which has veto power on all proposed rights. If they see Sharia that way, why is it impermissible for others to follow suit? On the other hand, the authors do conform to this idea of the indeterminacy of Sharia in the sense that they don't spell out what these exceptions are. 'Except for a Shari'a prescribed reason' could then mean one thing in Khartoum and another in Jakarta ... but then something so unspecified and mutable and culturally or geographically relative has no business in an international document 'on' human rights.

The standing of the Cairo Declaration is similarly difficult to figure out. It was 'Adopted and Issued at the Nineteenth Islamic Conference of Foreign Ministers in Cairo on 5 August 1990' and begins 'The Member States of the Organisation of the Islamic Conference' so it is an OIC document, but then the standing of the OIC is not altogether clear either. The OIC is simply a grouping of states with majority-Muslim populations, some of which have constitutions that declare Islam the religion of the state (Pakistan, Saudi Arabia, Malaysia) and others that don't – but then again it doesn't include India, which has the largest Muslim population in the world after Indonesia and Pakistan. It's a little difficult to know what such a grouping means since there are no equivalents for other religions. There is no Organization of Catholic Countries, or Buddhist or Hindu or anything else. The OIC isn't a military alliance like NATO or a universalist global grouping like the UN or a trade organization or a geographic entity like ASEAN or the African Union – the OIC is *sui generis*.

It is perhaps an attempt to match the influence and status of the Vatican, which is difficult to do in the absence of an official clerical hierarchy. The OIC perhaps compensates by adding state power into the mix. At any rate it seems fair to say that both organizations represent, at a minimum, the attempt to impose uniformity of belief and behaviour on vast dispersed populations, and to present a unified front to the rest of the world.

This generally is a goal of those in power, of course – some unity of belief and behaviour is a prerequisite of social peace, which in turn is a condition of commerce, prosperity, learning, culture, art, religion, of social capital of all kinds. Religion is a very powerful tool for inspiring unity (and thus also division). In the case of the OIC, in particular, religion perhaps plays this part in the absence of other, more desirable, less us–them kinds of mechanisms. The OIC member states are all relatively underdeveloped, and most of them are poor; those that are rich are rich because of oil, not because of scientific and technological advances. The *esprit de corps* of success is not an option for them as it is, for instance, for the European Union or NATO or the G8. Religion is the substitute glue.

The Vatican is in a somewhat similar situation. It is little heeded in once Catholic but now secular France; it is more significant in unprosperous Poland and in the recently unprosperous South – Portugal, Spain, Italy, which lagged behind the northern, Protestant countries, and in Latin America, Congo, the Philippines. This is at least suggestive.

There is some irony here, because of course most people in prosperous countries have nothing to do with technological innovation or scientific discovery, yet we enjoy a kind of reflected conceit merely by being citizens. People in less developed countries by the same token share in the generalized sense of inferiority even if they are in fact themselves intellectual giants.

Religion is then one way to compensate for national inferiority feelings, and as such, it tends to be pushed in more authoritarian dogmatic directions. A liberal watery permissive noncommittal sort of religion is by its nature less able to impose or inspire uniformity and solidarity in the group. Ideas of the sacred and the taboo, *haram* and *halal*, are part of the fervour and energy that foster group loyalty. The result seems to be that intense group loyalty is inseparable from dogmatism and authoritarianism.

It could be otherwise in theory; one can imagine Unitarians or Swedenborgians having as fierce a sense of the *ummah* as do cradle Catholics or Muslims, but in practice it doesn't seem to work that way. Group intensity and impervious dogmatism seem to go hand in hand. Perhaps this helps to explain dogmatic religion's hostility to the individual and individual rights.

The Iranian representative to the UN, as we've seen, told the UN

General Assembly in 1984 that certain concepts in the UDHR needed to be revised and that Iran 'recognized no authority or power but that of Almighty God.'[32] This is where dogmatism and authoritarianism enter the picture, and never leave. The UD, of course, never mentions God or any particular religion; this is a necessary condition of its aspiration to be universal. There is no universal concept of God; human beings don't agree on whether or not there is a God, nor on the nature of such a God, nor on what we know about it, nor on what it wants us to do, nor on how we know any of that. There is no universal epistemology of theism, so a declaration of human rights that was intended to be universal had no choice but to leave God out. There is no universal epistemology of human rights either, of course, which is why such a document is needed and why violations of it are so abundant, but the language of the agreement is thin enough that agreement is possible in principle if not (so far) in fact.

The invocation of 'no authority or power but that of Almighty God' introduces exactly the element that needs to be left out – the element of the absent, unknown, unknowable, unaccountable, arbitrary power – the tyrant, in short. It introduces the non-human authority/power into a declaration of *human* rights, where it doesn't belong. Earthquakes, hurricanes, tornadoes, volcanic eruptions have the power to demolish all human rights in an instant, but we don't make a virtue of that; on the contrary we do our best to prevent it.

The God added to the equation by Iran is the God that no one has ever seen, that does not make appearances, that sends no messages; this God is hidden, secretive, permanently and inviolably locked away from all living people; this fact alone is enough to disqualify it as an authority on human rights. It's a bad principle to expect humans to obey a putative god that is inaccessible and unknowable, just as it would be to expect us to obey human legislators who were equally hidden and unknowable and unaccountable.

More than that, there is little reason to think this unaccountable God is good or benevolent, and much reason to think it is not. If one reverse-engineers from the realities of life, or from Holy Books, or from both, there is much more reason to think God is indifferent or malevolent. If your God tells you to dash the Babylonian babies against the rocks (Psalm 137) or to bury a woman up to her waist and then stone her to death for adultery, then you are in exactly the same position as a soldier whose captain has issued an order to kill everyone in the village. The orders are wicked, and they must be refused.

This is not a new idea, to put it mildly. Plato and the author of the book of Job were much exercised by it. The piercing question that Socrates put to Euthyphro is the *locus classicus*:

> The point which I should first wish to understand is whether the pious or holy is beloved by the gods because it is holy, or holy because it is beloved of the gods.[33]

Taking holy to mean 'good', the question is all-important, yet the world is full of Euthyphros who never think to ask it. Does cruelty become good if a deity commands it? Or does cruelty remain wicked no matter who commands it?

The Universal Declaration says yes to the second question; the Cairo Declaration (without spelling it out) says yes to the first. This is the difference, and it could hardly be more consequential. The UD forbids cruelty and injustice, while the CD permits it 'within the framework of Shari'a'.[34]

The Vatican charter

What we are left with, then, is male clerics of all denominations demanding drastic limits on human rights, especially in the case of women – who are not allowed to be clerics. As we noted in Chapter 3, this is an obvious and egregious conflict of interest. The fact that it's a longstanding one doesn't make it any less so.

Consider the Vatican's 'Charter of the Rights of the Family': a charter of rights that is the product of an officially, adamantly all-male hierarchy, one that declares it heresy punishable by excommunication to claim that women too should be eligible for ordination[35] (which would *inter alia* give them a say in the rules that govern them).

The problem is inherent in the charter itself, before any provisions are even enunciated: the problem inheres in declaring 'rights' for group entities that can't, as such, have rights, because they don't have minds and so can't have desires or hopes. People of course want to make sacrifices for their families, but that does not translate to a right of the family. (Dependent children have rights which their parents have obligations to meet, but that is not the same thing as a right of the family.) It makes sense to talk of protections or exemptions or benefits for the family, but not rights. Rights are for people, one at a time; they can't be granted to groups or institutions (or corporations) without compromising or demolishing them for people.

So the Vatican's position is inimical to human rights, and in conflict with the very idea of human rights.

> One aspect of fundamental importance for the promotion of human rights is recognition of the 'rights of the family'. This implies the protection of marriage in the framework of 'human rights' and of family life as an objective of every juridical system. The *Charter of the Rights of the Family*, presented by the Holy See, implies the conception of the family as a subject that includes all its members. The family is thus a whole which should not be divided up when it is being dealt with by isolating its members – not even for reasons of social substitution which, although necessary in many cases, should never put the *family* as a subject in a marginal position.[36]

This notion of the family as a subject is the last refuge of those who want to keep women subordinate. Parents have responsibilities to their children, but that is a different matter from saying the family is a subject. A subject is an entity with subjective thoughts and feelings and experience, and thus an entity with a claim to rights. If the family is a subject, then perhaps it has rights which trump the rights of women within the family.

But the family is not such an entity, just as the community is not, the religion is not, the nation is not, the race is not. Subjects in that sense are and can be only individuals. Subjects are separate persons, and the separateness of persons means that it is unjust to sacrifice anyone's rights for a group.

'Defamation' of religion

From 1999 to 2005 the Organisation of the Islamic Conference annually presented a resolution to the UN Commission on Human Rights called 'Combating Defamation of Religions',[37] and every year the Commission adopted the resolution. By 2005 the Commission had become discredited, and in 2006 it was abolished by the UN General Assembly and replaced by the new Human Rights Council, which first met in March 2006. The OIC did not present a resolution condemning 'defamation of religion' that year, but in March 2007 it did. Roy Brown of the IHEU points out that the resolution is not 'actually aimed at helping prevent discrimination or violence against people on the basis of their religion or belief'.

> First, the resolution fails to define 'defamation'. It is a catch-all term intended to silence any criticism of religious practice or of laws based on religion – however pernicious. Secondly, it attempts to limit certain rights, including the right to freedom of expression, guaranteed under international human rights law. Thirdly, it fails to distinguish between religions and their followers. To criticize any aspect of Islam, for example, is seen as an attack on Muslims.[38]

This is another instantiation of the same problem, or mistake: transposing the idea of rights from people, as individuals, where they belong, to groups or institutions or abstractions, where they don't.

At a Congressional hearing on freedom of religion on 18 July

2008, Susan Bunn Livingstone, a former US State Department official who specialized in human rights issues, told the panel, 'They are using this discourse of 'defamation' to carve out any attention we would bring to a country. Abstractions like states and ideologies and religions are seen as more important than individuals. This is a moral failure.'[39]

The transfer of rights discourse from people to ideologies and religions is, pretty unmistakably, a way of dressing up coercion. It's a way of preventing free speech and hence free inquiry, which means it is a way of impeding the freedom of thought itself.

The idea that religions can be 'defamed' is clearly very sinister. Religions have vast power over the rules and customs of people; this undeniable fact means that religions absolutely must be wide open to criticism and dispute of all kinds. Religions shape the ways people are treated; religious laws often treat some people worse than secular laws do; this means that if anything religions have *less* claim to immunity than other institutions rather than more. We can demand minimal respect for *people* as a human right, but that demand cannot extend to any other entity without crippling our ability to critique, assess and reform our own conditions.

6 Mutilate in the Name of Purity

In Chapter 2, we noted that there is a common argument which holds that if religion is associated with some unfortunate practices then often it is because of the corrupting influence of social, political and cultural factors. This argument constitutes a challenge to the thesis of this book, which is that religion is in various ways bad for women. In particular, it opens up the possibility that what we take to be religious misogyny, as exemplified in the patterns of abuse and degradation we have detailed in the preceding chapters, is in fact a cultural, rather than religious, phenomenon.

Consider, for example, the case of forced marriage in Britain. Every year, some three hundred such marriages are reported to the government's Forced Marriage Unit, many more are known to social services, and still more go undetected. The phenomenon is overwhelmingly associated with families whose ethnic origins lie in South Asia. However, despite the importance of religious belief in the lives of British Muslims, Sikhs and Hindus, the line taken by the government, politicians and commentators is that forced marriage has nothing to do with religion. For example, in the year 2000, a government working group reported that it could find no major world faith that condones forced marriage, and stated that the misrepresentation of forced marriage as religious in nature should be challenged.[1] This assessment was confirmed in a later government report which emphasized, in bold text, that forced marriage cannot be justified on religious grounds, and that every faith condemns the practice.[2]

This view is also espoused by many of the people at the forefront of opposition to forced marriage in Britain. Ann Cryer MP, for example, who has campaigned against the practice for more than ten years, claims that forced marriage has little to do with religion, but rather is 'a brutal crime against humanity based on a mediaeval, patriarchal culture'.[3] Nazia Khanum, author of 'Forced marriage, family cohesion and community engagement', also emphasizes the patriarchal nature of the practice, arguing that it forms part of a 'system where parents believe they know what is best for their children'.[4]

The BBC takes a similar line. For example, an online resource devoted to the issue characterizes forced marriage as a cultural phenomenon, which

> affects men and women from all over the world, and across many cultural groups. The British Royal Family even has a history of it, as did many members of the British aristocracy in the past. It is important to understand that it is not limited to just a few cultural groups, although it does usually affect women who are of South Asian origin.[5]

The BBC is also at pains to point out, even in its straight news coverage, and more than a little disingenuously, that forced marriage is not the same as arranged marriage, presumably with the intention of making it clear that the problem is with a particular, 'distorted' cultural practice rather than with South Asian culture generally.

The trouble with this line that forced marriage is the product of culture rather than religion is that it tends towards incoherence under close scrutiny. It's not at all clear that it's even possible to separate religion from culture so cleanly that it makes sense to say one causes forced marriage while the other has nothing to do with it. Consider, for example, that Nazia Khanum, in her study of forced marriage in Luton, stresses the importance of religion in the lives of those groups most affected by the practice (in particular, Pakistanis and Bangladeshis): she cites as evidence Munira Mirza's study which found that 80 per cent of Muslims in Britain agree with the statement

'My religion is the most important thing in my life', compared with only 11 per cent of the general population of Britain who respond the same way.[6] Now hold this fact up against some of the factors identified by the Forced Marriage Unit as motivating forced marriage: controlling unwanted behaviour and sexuality, in particular the behaviour and sexuality of women; protecting 'family honour'; protecting 'misguided' religious ideals; preventing 'unsuitable' relationships; responding to peer group or family pressure; and so on.[7]

It is very hard to believe that the way religious people think and feel about issues of this kind is unaffected by their religious beliefs. The rules about what kind of sexual behaviour is 'unwanted' are spelled out by Islam and other religions, just as ideas of 'family honour' are shaped by religious norms. The fact that a religious ideal is misguided doesn't make it any less religious, and religious factors play a major role in determining what relationships are 'unsuitable' (for instance, in Islam a Muslim woman is forbidden to marry a non-Muslim man). It is entirely possible, then, that forced marriage is 'condemned by every faith' yet still causally bound up with beliefs that form part of a religious orthodoxy.

Religion and culture are not hermetically sealed parts of the social world, necessarily playing out in recognizably distinct forms of behaviour. Although it might make sense to treat these spheres as being conceptually specific – thus, for example, the sociologist Emile Durkheim defined religion as 'a unified system of beliefs and practices relative to sacred things' – whether or not particular behaviours are appropriately considered religious, or are causally related to beliefs and practices that are appropriately considered religious, is an empirical question, and the answer will partly be determined by the particular conception of religion that one employs.

In order to explore further some of the issues involved here, it is worth looking in some detail at female genital mutilation, a practice that is often considered to be cultural or traditional, rather than religious. In this way, it will be possible to determine whether or not the claim that the malign aspects of religion are a function of cultural distortions has more general merit than it seems to have in the case of forced marriage.

In Chapter 4, we discussed the issue of female genital mutilation (FGM) at some length, noting that in a number of African countries, the sexuality of women is policed and controlled by the mechanism of slicing off their genitalia and then sewing together what's left behind. This practice, termed infibulation, functions in the context of a symbolic nexus that valorizes notions of purity, cleanliness, virtue and fertility. Thus, for example, Janice Boddy argues that infibulation

> purifies, smooths, and makes clean the outer surface of the womb, the enclosure or hosh of the house of childbirth, it socializes or, if the phrase be permitted, culturalizes a woman's fertility. Through occlusion of the vaginal orifice, her womb, both literally and figuratively, becomes a social space: enclosed, impervious, virtually impenetrable.[8]

However, although the practice is bound up in symbolism, myth and ritual, a frequent claim is that infibulation, and FGM more generally, are not religious in character. Carla Obermeyer, for example, on the basis of a comprehensive review of the FGM literature, concludes that there is 'no unequivocal link' between religion and FGM.[9] A number of things tend to be said in favour of this view.

First, there is fairly convincing evidence that the practice of FGM predates the emergence of Christianity and Islam. According to some scholars, the first reference to female 'circumcision' occurs in Herodotus' *Histories* as far back as the fifth century BCE.[10] Certainly, a Greek papyrus dated 163 BCE indicates that the circumcision of girls prior to their marriage was customary among the Egyptians of that period. By the first century of the common era, the practice was (relatively) well known. The Greek geographer Strabo, for example, stated in his magnum opus, *Geographica*, published in 23 CE, that:

> One of the customs most zealously observed among the Egyptians is this,
> that they rear every child that is born, and circumcise the males, and
> excise the females ...[11]

This, and other similar evidence, has led to the fairly common,
though disputed, view that FGM likely emerged first in Egypt and the
Nile Valley before spreading throughout the African continent.[12]

Second, there is no straightforward correspondence between
religious belief and the prevalence of FGM. Although it is true that
FGM is predominantly found in Muslim countries, it is also true that
most Muslims do not practise it, and that it is also practised by non-
Muslims, such as Egypt's Coptic Christians.

Third, there is little, if any, support for FGM in the 'sacred' texts and
traditions of the major monotheistic religions. Neither the Bible nor
the Koran talks about the practice explicitly, and although there are
two or three ahadith in the Muslim tradition that seem to support
FGM, these are generally considered to be of dubious authenticity.
Similarly with Judaism: neither the Talmud nor the Torah mandates
FGM, and indeed the practice is virtually non-existent among Jews
(the one exception being the Beta Israel of Ethiopia).

Taken together these points seem to support an argument that
FGM is a traditional, cultural phenomenon that exists side-by-side
with whatever religion happens to be dominant in the areas where it
has always been practised – for example, Islam in Egypt and
Christianity in Kenya. According to this view, there is an accom-
modation between FGM and religion, but there is little or nothing in
the nature of FGM itself that is religious, as is evidenced by the fact
that in those parts of the world where FGM has never been practised,
it is viewed as being incompatible with the prevailing religious
orthodoxy.

At first sight, this is an attractive argument. It appears to make
sense of the fact – if indeed it is a fact – that FGM is not prescribed by
any world religion, and it also explains why FGM does not exist in
most parts of the world, even in many parts where religion is woven

into the fabric of everyday life. However, on closer examination it becomes clear that the argument is both empirically suspect and logically flawed.

On the empirical side of things, the first thing to say is that while there is fairly convincing evidence that FGM predates Christianity and Islam, we actually know very little about the origins and development of the practice. Things we don't know with any certainty include: where and when the practice first emerged; whether there was one point of origin or whether it arose independently among different groups on multiple occasions;[13] how its various forms developed; whether the practice existed in Arabia prior to the rise of Islam; and what kinds of meanings have been attached to it by its practitioners.

This lack of knowledge is a problem for the idea that FGM was already an established cultural practice when Christianity and Islam arrived on the scene. In particular, a number of alternative scenarios, consistent with the evidence that some form of FGM had existed in ancient Egypt, present themselves. For example, it is possible that FGM had been a sporadic and inconsequential practice, waxing and waning according to fashion, until the major monotheistic religions made their presence felt in Africa and the Middle East, providing the scaffolding required to build a more permanent tradition. Equally, it is possible that the meanings attached to FGM have been so transformed by the impact of religion that it would be a mistake to think the modern version of the practice is identical to the ancient one. This is not to argue that either of these scenarios is likely to be true, or even that either is more likely to be true than the idea that FGM is a long-established traditional practice existing alongside religion proper. It is simply to argue that we don't know enough about the origins and development of the practice to reach *any* firm conclusions.

There are also problems with the idea that there is little, if any, support for FGM in the 'sacred' texts and traditions of the major monotheistic religions. Here it is necessary to make a distinction between what is true of Judaism and Christianity, and what is true of Islam. It is generally accepted that there is nothing in Judaism or Christianity to suggest that the practice of FGM has ever played a part in either religion. It is simply not on their radar. However, this is not true of Islam.

The key point here is that the Koran is not the only source Muslims rely on for guidance in matters of faith and practice. In particular, there is a long tradition in Islam – although it is contested – of accepting the ahadith and sirah (together, the *sunnah*) as having religious authority. According to Muhammad Salim al-Awwa, the Secretary General of the International Union for Muslim Scholars, Islamic law is derived from four sources: the Koran; the *sunnah*; scholarly consensus; and analogy (from previous cases and rulings).[14] It is in the extra-Koranic sources that support for FGM is found.

Classical Muslim scholars, such as Tabari, locate the origin of FGM in a dispute within Abraham's household. They report that Abraham's wife, Sarah, in a fit of jealousy, threatened to maim Hagar, the mother of Abraham's son Ishmael (who is considered the father of the Arabs). Abraham warned Sarah to do no more than 'circumcise' Hagar, which she proceeded to do, while Hagar slept, thereby establishing the practice among the descendents of the Arabs.

Although this tale is apocryphal, and we can't be certain whether FGM existed in the Hijaz before Islam was established, a number of ahadith suggest that it was an extant practice, and that Muhammad viewed it in a favourable light. The most frequently cited, found in the *Sunan* of Abu Dawood, one of the six authentic ahadith collections, states that the Prophet advised a female 'circumciser' that 'circumcision' was permitted, but that she should not cut excessively, since that way is more 'pleasant' for the woman and preferred by the husband. Another ahadith holds that Muhammad stated that 'circumcision' is *sunna* (recommended) for men and a 'sign of respect' for women. And a third ahadith instructs that if two 'circumcised' parts (of a man and a woman) come into contact, then ablution is obligatory (implying that women were 'circumcised').

These traditions are much disputed among Islamic scholars. For example, al-Awwa argues that:

> it is clear that in true sunna there is no evidence that female circumcision is endorsed, that all the hadith on female circumcision used as evidence are poor in authenticity and cannot serve as the basis for a religious ruling, and that the practice is nothing other than a custom which Islam left for time and for progress in medicine to refine or abolish.[15]

Whether or not al-Awwa is right about this is not what is significant here. The fact that these are matters of scholarly dispute is enough on its own to establish that there is little justification for the blanket assertion that there is no support for FGM in the texts of the major monotheistic religions. Consider, for example, that Gad-al-Haq, the Great Sheikh of Al-Azhar University, arguably the Muslim world's premier centre of learning, issued a detailed *fatwa* in 1981, in which he insisted, *contra* al-Awwa, that FGM should not be abandoned, that Muhammad's teachings couldn't simply be tossed aside in favour of the teaching of another, and that parents who did not get their daughters 'circumcised' were not doing their duty. He added that: 'If the people of a region refuse to practice male and female circumcision, the chief of the state can declare war upon them.'[16]

Sheikh Yusuf al-Qaradawi, whom we met in Chapter 3, and who is considered by many to be a moderate conservative, has also offered qualified support for the practice of FGM:

> the most moderate opinion and the most likely one to be correct is in favor of practicing circumcision in the moderate Islamic way indicated in some of the Prophet's hadiths – even though such hadiths are not confirmed to be authentic. It is reported that the Prophet ... said to a midwife: 'Reduce the size of the clitoris but do not exceed the limit, for that is better for her health and is preferred by husbands'. The hadith indicates that circumcision is better for a woman's health and it enhances her conjugal relation with her husband. It's noteworthy that the Prophet's saying 'do not exceed the limit' means do not totally remove the clitoris.[17]

Views of this kind are not nearly as unusual among Muslim scholars as one might gather from reading recent literature on FGM. In fact, it is entirely possible that majority Muslim opinion comes out in favour of FGM. Sami A. Aldeeb, for example, notes that numerous Muslim authors condemn the practice, but argues that the majority consider it a 'meritorious act' rather than simply a custom, basing their opinion on Muhammad's words. He adds:

> Those Muslims who practice female circumcision think that it is part of their religion. The decision not to circumcise a daughter has serious social consequences ... In the Egyptian countryside, the matron who practices female circumcision delivers a certificate for the marriage ... El-Masry relates the words of an Egyptian midwife who had circumcised more than 1000 girls. According to her, fathers who oppose the excision of their daughters should be lynched because in effect they accept the girls becoming prostitutes, which she sees as the only recourse for unmarriageable women.[18]

Happily, we do not need to take sides in this debate about whether or not the *sunnah* endorses FGM. As became clear in Chapter 2, arguments about how religious texts and traditions should properly be interpreted are often futile in the extreme. The significant point here is that there is no justification for the pretence that this is a settled issue. It is not, and even if it were, it would remain an open possibility that it might become unsettled again at some point in the future.

The final point worth making about the evidence generally offered for the claim that there is no link between religion and FGM has to do with the demographics of the practice. A major issue for those who wish to claim that FGM is 'nothing other than a custom' is that it occurs overwhelmingly in Muslim societies. The standard response is to point out that it is also practised by non-Muslims – for example, Christians in places such as Kenya and Côte d'Ivoire, Coptic Christians in Egypt, and the Beta Israel Jews in Ethiopia – and that in most parts of the world Muslims are not genitally mutilated.

The idea seems to be that since non-Muslims practise FGM, and since many Muslims do not practise it, there can be no causal relationship between Islam (specifically) and FGM. However, this is a flawed argument. Consider for a moment the link between cigarette smoking and lung cancer. Most people who get lung cancer smoke; some people who get lung cancer do not smoke; and many people who smoke, never get lung cancer. This set of relationships is structurally identical to that which exists between FGM and Islam: most people who practise FGM are Muslims; some people who practise FGM are non-Muslims; and many Muslims do not practise FGM. We know there is a causal relationship between smoking and lung cancer. Therefore, it follows that the fact that non-Muslims practise FGM, and many Muslims do not practise it, *does not rule out* a causal link between Islam and FGM.

However, it is important to understand that it is not ruled in here either. The significant point is that we cannot infer causality from these broad relationships: on their own, they tell us little about the link between Islam and FGM. The only thing it is possible to say with any certainty is that a causal link remains an open possibility.

In fact, it will be very difficult to establish the existence of such a link – or indeed to show that there is no such link – just by looking at statistical data on the prevalence of FGM. To get a sense of the complexities involved here, it is worth briefly considering some of the findings of a UNICEF study titled 'Female Genital Mutilation/Cutting: A Statistical Exploration', which was published in 2005. It has this to say about the link between religion and FGM:

> While religion can help to explain FGM/C distribution in many countries, the relationship is not consistent. In six of the countries where data on religion are available – Benin, Côte d'Ivoire, Ethiopia, Ghana, Kenya and Senegal – Muslim population groups are more likely to practise FGM/C than Christian groups. In five countries there seems [sic] to be no significant differences, while in Niger, Nigeria and the United Republic of Tanzania the prevalence is greater among Christian groups.
>
> Looking at religion independently, it is not possible to establish a general association with FGM/C status. The most marked differences can

be observed in Benin, Côte d'Ivoire, Ghana and Senegal. In Côte d'Ivoire, for example, 79 per cent of Muslim women have undergone FGM/C, compared with 16 per cent of Christian women.[19]

Reading this, one might be tempted to conclude that there is a weak causal link between Islam and FGM. In six of the fourteen countries surveyed, Muslims are more likely to practise FGM than Christians, compared with only three out of the fourteen countries where it is the other way around. However, on closer examination, it becomes clear that these data actually tell us very little about the relationship between religion – whether Islam or Christianity – and FGM. This is the case for a number of reasons; the reasons are a little technical, but they are worth talking about briefly.

First, a comparison between Muslim population groups and Christian population groups, if it tells us anything at all beyond simple correlations, will tell us only about the link between FGM and each particular religion *relative* to each other. Certainly, it doesn't tell us anything about the causal relationship between religion generally and FGM. Analogously, we're not going to learn much about the causal link between smoking and lung cancer if we only compare lung cancer rates for smokers against lung cancer rates for people who have been exposed to asbestos, for example. Even if we find out that 80 per cent of both groups develop lung cancer, we haven't discovered anything about causality, since we have no data from a control group – i.e. people who don't smoke and haven't been exposed to asbestos – against which we can compare these figures. Similarly, we won't find anything out about the causal relationship between religion and FGM by looking only at Muslims and Christians, since we will have no idea what FGM rates would have been in the absence of religion.

Second, if you're dealing in broad statistical comparisons between groups within a society then it is very difficult to isolate all the factors that potentially play a role in determining the rates of FGM. For example, the UNICEF study cited above shows that 79 per cent of

Muslim women compared to only 16 per cent of Christian women have undergone FGM in Côte d'Ivoire. It is tempting to conclude that this disparity must be a function of the difference between Islam and Christianity. But suppose the rate of FGM is affected by factors such as level of education, the urban/rural divide, income level, and so on. If so, then perhaps it is these factors rather than religion that explain the difference in FGM rates between Muslims and Christians in Côte d'Ivoire. We simply have no way of knowing.

Third, any attempt to look at the relationship between religion and FGM by comparing statistical data for groups of believers with non-believers will confront enormous difficulties. In particular, it is unlikely to be possible to survey enough non-believers in those countries where FGM is common to make meaningful comparisons.[20] Moreover, even if this turns out to be possible, non-belief will almost certainly co-vary with other factors that likely play a role in determining the rate of FGM – for example, level of education, income, cultural milieu, and so on – which will make it incredibly hard to isolate belief as an independent variable (where FGM is the dependent variable).

Problems of this kind mean that while empirical data are helpful for the purposes of estimating the extent of FGM, and for allowing us to discern patterns of correlation, they are much less useful for the job of determining whether religion is causally, rather than contingently, linked to FGM. The task then is to show why, in the absence of compelling empirical data, it remains reasonable to conclude that the practice of FGM is intimately bound up with religion and religious belief.

A good way to approach this task is to look again at the argument we identified earlier as tending to be advanced by people who wish to deny that FGM has anything to do with religion. It holds that FGM is a traditional practice that predates Christianity and Islam; that it is not prescribed by any world religion; and that it continues to be practised today only in those parts of the world – primarily in Africa – where it has always been practised. It follows, therefore, or so it is claimed, that FGM is a traditional, cultural practice that has little to do with religion.

We have already seen that this argument is predicated on claims that are empirically suspect. Thus, for example, we noted that the assertion that FGM predates Christianity and Islam is rendered almost empty by our lack of knowledge about its origins and development; and that the contention that FGM is not prescribed by any world religion is undermined by the fact that many Muslim scholars – perhaps a majority – argue that it is a 'meritorious act'. However, there is another point worth making here, which is that regardless of the truth or otherwise of its premises, the argument doesn't work. Even if one grants its factual claims, it fails to establish that FGM has little, or nothing, to do with religion.

Consider, for example, that there is nothing contradictory in asserting that both the following propositions are true:

1.   FGM predates religion.
2.   A necessary condition of the existence of FGM in a particular locale is that it predates religion in that locale.

And yet that it is also true that:

1.   Religion, and in particular Islam, is part of the causal story of the existence and persistence of FGM in the present day.

It is worth saying something briefly about why there is no contradiction here. A medical analogy will help to make things clear. Let's suppose that a patient is suffering from a simple bacterial infection. Unfortunately, it is misdiagnosed as a rare virus, which requires a bone marrow transplant to be successfully treated. Before the transplant takes place, the patient undergoes total body irradiation, which has the (intended) effect of destroying her immune system. However, the misdiagnosis means that the result of this treatment is that the bacterial infection spreads rapidly around her body. Consequently, unable to fight off the infection, she is bound to experience multiple organ failure and death.

This scenario has the following structure:

1. The simple bacterial infection predates the total body irradiation.

2. A necessary condition of the particular course taken by the patient's rapidly advancing illness and impending death is that the infection predated the total body irradiation.

And yet:

1. Total body irradiation is part of the causal story of what has happened to this patient: the infection is ravaging her body because her immune system has been destroyed by the treatment.

It is clear, then, that there is nothing contradictory in claiming both that a necessary condition of the patient's current predicament is that the bacterial infection was present prior to her undergoing total body irradiation; and also that this treatment is part of the causal story of what has happened to her. Similarly, there is nothing contradictory in claiming that a necessary condition of the existence of FGM is that it predates religion; and also that religion is part of the causal story of extant FGM.

This is a logical point, of course. It shows that sceptics about the link between religion and FGM are wrong to think that a causal relationship is ruled out by the fact – if it is a fact – that FGM predates the major monotheistic religions. However, this is not an argument in favour of a causal link, merely an argument for its logical possibility. To make an argument for a causal link requires a different approach.

A common thread running through this book is that religion can come to permeate every aspect of the lives of women. Thus, for example, in Chapter 4 we saw how the strictures of Wahhabism define the lives of women in Saudi Arabia: Saudi women are not allowed to drive; they are forced to wear the *abaya*, which a BBC reporter described as 'an all-enveloping black cloak that turns the women of the Gulf into mournful ghosts';[21]and they need permission from a male guardian before travelling anywhere. Similarly, in Chapter 1 we noted that women in Iran risk attracting the wrath of the religious police if they so much as inadvertently expose their hair; that the Taliban in Afghanistan forbade women to laugh out loud and to wear shoes that clicked; and that in countries where the Catholic Church is strong, such as Colombia, Chile and Poland, access to abortion services is either illegal or severely restricted.

The ubiquity of religion in the lives of believers, men and women alike, is also indicated by a multitude of survey data. A Pew Global Attitudes report, published in 2008, found that in 17 of 23 countries a majority of people say religion is very or somewhat important to them personally. In the predominantly Muslim countries Egypt, Jordan, Pakistan and Indonesia more than 95 per cent of people consider religion to be personally significant.[22] This high level of religiosity is reflected in patterns of religious observance: large majorities in all Muslim publics pray at least once a day and fast most days during Ramadan.[23]

Similar patterns of religiosity have been found by other surveys. An earlier Pew study, published in 2002, showed that no fewer than 80 per cent of respondents in *every* African country surveyed rated religion as being *very* important to them personally.[24] A 2007 Gallup survey found that nearly two-thirds of Egyptians think that Sharia – defined as Islam's religious principles, values and ethics – should be the only source of legislation; and 90 per cent think that it should be *a* source of legislation (compared with only 3 per cent who think otherwise).[25] A 2006 study found that Muslims in Britain, Spain, Germany, France, Pakistan, Jordan, Egypt, Turkey and Nigeria identify themselves primarily as Muslims rather than as citizens of their own countries (the only exception being Indonesia where a small majority of Muslims see themselves first as Indonesian).[26]

The point here is that in many countries, including those such as Egypt, Nigeria and Somalia where FGM is almost universal, religion is omnipresent. It is the pervasive social monitor, spying on behaviour, enforcing rules and punishing disobedience. It is also the ground of much thought: it is intentionally intrusive and ubiquitous, so that people struggle to have any thoughts that are not coloured by their religion. At the extreme it is like bindweed or kudzu, sending out shoots and runners faster than anyone can cut them back, until it buries the landscape and chokes off all other growth.

This is manifest in the way that religion is intimately linked to the values espoused by believers. A study conducted in 2007 found widespread agreement throughout Africa, Asia and the Middle East that belief in God is necessary for morality.

> (I)n all 10 African countries included in the study, at least seven-in-ten respondents agree with the statement 'It is necessary to believe in God in order to be moral and have good values.' In Egypt, no one in the sample of 1,000 people disagrees. Out of the 1,000 Jordanians interviewed, only one person suggests it is possible to not believe in God and still be a moral person. In the four predominantly Muslim Asian countries – Indonesia, Bangladesh, Pakistan and Malaysia – huge majorities also believe morality requires faith in God.[27]

There is also strong evidence that the attitudes people have about particular moral issues are determined (at least in part) by the intensity and character of their religious commitment. Thus, for example, a recent Gallup poll found that only 4 per cent of Muslims in London think homosexual acts are morally acceptable, compared to 28 per cent of religious Americans and 81 per cent of the French public (generally considered to be among the most secular in the world). This general pattern is repeated for attitudes towards abortion (rated as 'morally acceptable' by 10 per cent of London Muslims, 22 per cent of religious Americans and 77 per cent of the French public), pornography (rated as 'morally acceptable' by 4 per cent of London Muslims, 7 per cent of Paris Muslims and 52 per cent of the French public) and premarital sex (rated as 'morally acceptable' by 11 per cent of London Muslims, 38 per cent of religious Americans and 88 per cent of the French public).[28]

There is also a striking homogeneity of opinion among the

citizens of countries that score high for religiosity. For example, the most recent Pew report has this to say about the way Jews are viewed by people in Arab countries:

> Negative views are most common in the three predominantly Arab nations included in the survey. Only 2% of Lebanese have a favorable opinion of Jews, while 97% hold an unfavorable view, including 99% among both Sunni and Shia Muslims, as well as 95% of the country's Christians. In Jordan (96% unfavorable) and Egypt (95%) opinions also are nearly unanimously negative. This pattern is not new, however; previous Pew surveys in these three countries have found 95% or more expressing unfavorable views of Jews.[29]

Hostile attitudes towards Jews are also found in the other mainly Muslim countries included in the survey. Fewer than one in ten people in Pakistan and Turkey, for instance, express favourable opinions.[30]

This homogeneity of opinion extends into the moral sphere. The citizens of African countries are almost unanimous in believing homosexuality to be unacceptable. According to one study, 89 per cent of people in Côte d'Ivoire think that homosexuality should be rejected by society; in Ghana, the figure is 94 per cent; in Tanzania, 95 per cent; in Kenya, Uganda, Senegal, Ethiopia, Nigeria and Mali it is even higher.[31] Not surprisingly, many of these countries also have laws prohibiting homosexual behaviour, with punishments ranging from fines to the death penalty (as sanctioned in Nigeria, for example, by Sharia).

Of course, this is not to say that correlation equals causality. It is mistaken to suppose that the mere association of religiosity with particular behaviours, beliefs and values is an indication that religion is causally implicated in those behaviours, beliefs and values. Certainly, for example, it is easy to imagine someone such as Karen Armstrong insisting that Islam is tolerant of Judaism, and that the hostile attitudes that Muslim publics express about Jews have nothing to do with either religion, but rather are a function of the conflict in the Middle East and in particular the injustices suffered by the Palestinian people.

Needless to say, the substantive point here is partly right. It would be quite absurd to think that religion is the whole explanation of the attitudes that Jordanians have towards Jews; or Nigerians towards homosexuality; or religious Americans towards premarital sex; or the Taliban towards women. But equally, it would be absurd to suppose that religion has nothing to do with these attitudes, that it is not part of their explanation. More generally, it is entirely implausible to think that the behaviour, beliefs and values of people who state that religion is very important to them, who are religiously observant, who think that a belief in God is a prerequisite of moral behaviour, who self-identify in terms of their religion rather than nationality, who reside in countries suffused with religious ritual and imagery, and who live in terms of the minutiae of religious law, have nothing to do with religion. It is the equivalent of insisting that the Pope or Grand Mufti is wearing no clothes when in fact he is decked out in full religious regalia.

This point brings us back to the issue of female genital mutilation. The argument in favour of a causal link between religion and FGM is simply that it is absurd to think a practice so bound up in symbolism, myth and ritual, one that is explicitly part of a discourse of purity, virtue and virginity and that is prevalent almost exclusively in societies notable for their high levels of religiosity, might somehow be hermetically sealed off from the influence of religion. This argument does not require that FGM is endorsed or sanctioned by religious texts and traditions, nor that it finds support among imams and priests (although both these things might be true); simply that its prevalence and/or survival is in some way dependent upon the beliefs and practices that constitute religion.

Ayaan Hirsi Ali, for example, argues that FGM is popular in Muslim countries because it is believed to reduce the sexual feelings of women, with the consequence that it helps to preserve virginity.

> In Somalia, like many countries across Africa and the Middle East, little girls are made 'pure' by having their genitals cut out ... [T]he practice is always justified in the name of Islam. Uncircumcised girls will be possessed by devils, fall into vice and perdition, and become whores. Imams never discourage the practice: it keeps girls pure.[32]

Hirsi Ali's argument here is similar to the argument about religion and forced marriage that we outlined at the beginning of this chapter. The motivation for FGM is not always *explicitly* religious, but almost always it is motivated by factors that have a religious dimension. In particular, as we saw in Chapters 3 and 4, conceptions of femininity, appropriate sexual behaviour, the importance of purity, modesty and virtue, and the proper relations between the sexes, all of which form part of the common narrative of FGM, are fundamentally religious in nature. Thus, it is entirely possible for FGM to be condemned by every religion – although in fact it is not – and yet still to be causally bound up with beliefs that form part of a religious orthodoxy.

Moreover, even if FGM were not linked to this constellation of (partly) religious beliefs about femininity and purity, religion would still be fundamental to the survival of the practice. Take the case of Mali, for example, where it is estimated that more than 90 per cent of women undergo FGM. A US State department report describes the attitudes and beliefs surrounding FGM in Mali as follows:

> This practice is so deeply rooted in tradition and culture that any challenge to it runs into strong social opposition and repercussions. Women who have not been subjected to one of the procedures or parents who refuse to subject their daughters to it face social pressures and potential ostracism from society.
>
> Some Bambara and Dogon [Mali ethnic groups] believe that if the clitoris comes in contact with the baby's head during birth, the child will die. It is their deeply held belief that both the female and the male sex exist within each person at birth and it is necessary to rid the female body of vestiges of maleness to overcome any sexual ambiguity. The clitoris represents the male element in a young girl while the foreskin represents

the female element in a young boy. Both must be removed to clearly demarcate the sex of the person.[33]

Although ostensibly a description of a traditional practice, it is possible to see traces of the influence of Islam – overwhelmingly, Mali's dominant religion – in this account, particularly in the concern with the purity of sexual identity. However, even if one leaves this aside, and treats these beliefs as purely traditional, religion still plays a role here. Specifically, it underpins the worldview, and provides the cultural context, within which the extra-rational mythology associated with FGM can thrive. To put it simply, a culture that is steeped in the supernatural constitutes fertile ground for practices such as FGM, which depend for their sustenance on an extra-rational mythology, to flourish. In Weberian terms, there is an 'elective affinity' between religion and symbolism, myth and ritual that surrounds FGM, which holds even where the practice is not specifically linked to the constellation of beliefs about femininity and purity that is central to Islam and Christianity.[34]

The general point here is that it simply isn't possible to pull religion and culture apart from each other when we're dealing with societies – or, indeed, sub-cultures – characterized by high levels of religiosity. Such is the interpenetration of these spheres that they become in effect different names for the same thing: the fabric of life, the deep background of virtually every thought and loyalty, the heart of a heartless world, the motivation for pretty much everything. Religion *is* culture, and often the upshot is that women and their bodies and their genitals are public property and God's property. There is no succour, then, for religious apologists in the thought that the terrible things done in the name of religion are caused by malign cultural or social forces, since religion inevitably leaves its fingerprints all over the 'distortions' that lead to practices such as FGM, forced marriage, child marriage and honour killings.

7 Islam, Islamophobia and Risk

It will not have escaped the notice of the attentive reader, and perhaps even the inattentive reader, that as we've detailed the crimes of religion against women, Islam has been indicted more often than the other members of the religion community. Honour killings, female genital mutilation, forced marriage, child marriage, ferocious control of female sexuality, restrictions on personal freedom, medieval dress codes, and the like, are all disproportionately associated with Islam. It is not as though we've ignored the sins of other religions – we've looked at FLDS patriarchy, the Catholic Church's stance on abortion, the Haredi obsession with female modesty, Southern Baptist 'complementarianism', Ghana's witchcraft 'problem', Hinduism's cruelty to widows, and so on – but there's no denying that Islam is leading the pack in the misogyny stakes.

Of course, such a statement will be greeted with howls of horror and derision by ecumenicists, Islamists, anthropologists, counter-hegemonic leftists, and post-colonialist feminists, so it is necessary to make a number of things clear from the outset.

The first thing to say is that our criticisms are directed towards Islam as a religion, not towards individual Muslims (or indeed Christians or Jews or Hindus), and also (obviously) we are not using Islam as a proxy in order to attack particular ethnic groups. It should not be necessary to point these things out, but unfortunately, as we will see later, it has become a lazy habit to equate criticism of Islam with racism or a general antipathy towards the unfamiliar Other.

We are aware that Islam is not a single homogeneous entity –
which would be a very odd thing to think given that the Sunnis and
Shia have been slaughtering each other periodically for over a
thousand years – but rather a complex social phenomenon with
differing traditions and tendencies. It is also true that the Koran is
subject to multiple interpretations (some of them more acceptable
than others), that Islam experienced a 'Golden Age' or Enlightenment
long before any such thing occurred in the West, that Andalusian
Islam was (relatively) progressive, that a vanishingly small proportion
of Muslims are terrorists, and that there is a nascent Islamic feminist
movement. All this is very nice, but unfortunately doesn't alter the
fact that in many places in the present day Islam is terribly bad for
women.

It is additionally worth making it clear that people sometimes
criticize Islam for entirely unconscionable reasons. The British
National Party's newly found anti-Islamic feminism is laughable,
obviously, and there's also some evidence to suggest that violence
against Muslims has increased since 9/11. However, although this is
deplorable, it tells us nothing about the substance of the issues we're
dealing with here. It is entirely possible, after all, that the BNP's
criticism of Islam is motivated by racism, that it is intended to stir up
racial hatred, and yet that it is also by and large right. The fact that
good people are subject to physical and verbal assault because of
their religion tells us nothing at all about the validity or moral
character of their beliefs.

Part of the reason it is necessary to say these things is that
accusations of 'Islamophobia' are increasingly being employed in an
attempt to defuse and silence criticism of Islam. Although there is no
generally accepted definition of the term – which is hardly surprising
given that its primary use is rhetorical – there have been a number of
attempts to spell out what it involves. Perhaps the most influential is
to be found in a Runnymede Trust report titled 'Islamophobia: A
Challenge for Us All', which was published in 1997.

According to this report, Islamophobia is 'an outlook or worldview involving an unfounded dread and dislike of Muslims', which has the following characteristics:[35]

- Islam is seen as a single monolithic bloc, unresponsive to new realities.
- Islam is seen as not having any aims or values in common with other cultures, not affected by them, and not influencing them.
- Islam is seen as inferior to the West – barbaric, irrational, primitive and sexist.
- Islam is seen as violent, supportive of terrorism, and engaged in 'a clash of civilizations'.
- Islam is seen as a political ideology, used for political or military advantage.
- Criticisms made by Islam of 'the West' are rejected out of hand.
- Hostility towards Islam is used to justify discriminatory practices towards Muslims and exclusion of Muslims from mainstream society.
- Anti-Muslim hostility is accepted as natural and 'normal'.

Unfortunately, though influential, this conception is badly flawed. Not least, it pathologizes a number of beliefs that are almost certainly true. For example, it is not unreasonable to think that Islam is irrational. Like any religion, it is founded on truth-claims that don't get anywhere near satisfying the criteria for rational justifiability. Anthony Grayling puts it like this:

> Religious belief of all kinds shares the same intellectual respectability, evidential base, and rationality as belief in the existence of fairies.
>
> This remark outrages the sensibilities of those who have deep religious convictions and attachments, and they regard it as insulting. But the truth is that everyone takes this attitude about all but one (or a very few) of the gods that have ever been claimed to exist.[36]

Certainly then most atheists are going to think that Islam is irrational. However, this judgement has nothing to do with prejudice or 'unfounded dread', even if it does lead to the further thought that

Western societies that confine religion to the private sphere are 'superior' to Islamic societies (which do not).

Similarly with the claim that Islam is sexist. Even if one views Islam in its best light – ignoring honour killings, child marriage, FGM, and the like – it is still a long way from espousing sexual equality in its core teachings. Consider, for example, that the Koran contains the following lines (as we noted in Chapter 2):

> Men have authority over women because God has made the one superior to the other, and because they spend their wealth to maintain them. Good women are obedient. They guard their unseen parts because God has guarded them. If you fear high-handedness from your wives, remind them [of the teachings of God], then ignore them when you go to bed, then hit them'. (Koran: 4.34)

It is not necessary to be a particularly radical feminist to think that there is something sexist in this kind of talk. Needless to say, the Islam apologetics industry will dispute the meaning and import of these words. But, in this context, that is neither here nor there. There is plenty of textual, historical and empirical evidence to support the view that Islam is sexist. As we saw in Chapter 2, not everybody agrees that this is what the evidence shows, but presumably very few people will argue that there is no case for Islam to answer. In this situation, it is absurd to think that people are prejudiced simply because they come down on the side of the claim that Islam *is* sexist (any more than they would be prejudiced if they think that there is evidence to support a judgement that Christianity is sexist).

A similar kind of argument can be levelled against the idea that it is Islamophobic to see Islam 'as violent, supportive of terrorism, and engaged in "a clash of civilisations"'. Part of the problem here is that it isn't exactly clear what this means. Clearly if you think that every Muslim is violent and supports terrorism then your views are verging towards the pathological. However, there are other ways of cashing out this statement where it would be much more reasonable to assent. Certainly there is textual evidence – in particular, the distinction between lesser and greater jihad – to support the claim that Islam countenances violence in certain, *not clearly defined*, circumstances; and there are legitimate worries about Islamic terrorism and the relationship between Western and Islamic countries.

There is some polling data that makes for interesting reading when one considers the issue of Islam and violence. It shows that there is fairly widespread support for suicide bombings among Arab and Nigerian Muslims,[37] and also, somewhat paradoxically, that:

> Worries about Islamic extremism are pervasive among nations with sizeable Muslim populations. Majorities in seven of the eight nations where this question was asked are concerned about the rise of Islamic extremism in the world today.
>
> Seven-in-ten or more are concerned in Indonesia, Pakistan, Tanzania and Lebanon. And more than half of Pakistanis and Tanzanians are very concerned …
>
> Similar proportions say they are concerned about Islamic extremism *in their countries*. Majorities in seven of eight countries are very or somewhat concerned about the rise of extremism in their country, and worries are especially widespread in Lebanon (78%), Pakistan (72%) and Egypt (72%).[38]

So the question arises whether non-Western Muslims who are worried about Islamic extremism are guilty of Islamophobia? If they are not, then it would seem perverse to claim that similar fears in the West are necessarily a manifestation of anti-Islamic prejudice, especially since things such as the level of anti-Semitism and support for suicide bombers in mainly Muslim countries *are* worth worrying about.

There is a counter-argument to these points: that Islamophobia is not identical to a particular set of critical attitudes, but rather is *indicated* by it (where Islamophobia is defined as an 'unfounded dread and dislike of Muslims', for example). However, the trouble with this argument is that the concept simply isn't employed in this kind of nuanced way. Rather, it is used as catch-all pejorative designed to

neutralize any criticism of Islam. Kenan Malik, writing in 2005, makes
the point like this:

> 'Islamophobia' has become not just a description of anti-Muslim prejudice
> but also a prescription for what may or may not be said about Islam. Every
> year, the Islamic Human Rights Commission organises a mock awards
> ceremony for its 'Islamophobe of the Year'. Last year there were two British
> winners. One was the BNP's Nick Griffin. The other? *Guardian* columnist
> Polly Toynbee. Toynbee's defence of secularism and women's rights, and
> criticism of Islam, was, it declared, unacceptable. Isn't it absurd, I asked the
> IHRC's Massoud Shadjareh, to equate a liberal anti-racist like Polly Toynbee
> with the leader of a neo-fascist party. Not at all, he suggested. 'There is a
> difference between disagreeing and actually dismissing certain ideologies
> and certain principles. We need to engage and discuss. But there's a limit
> to that.' It is difficult to know what engagement and discussion could
> mean when leading Muslim figures seem unable to distinguish between
> liberal criticism and neo-fascist attacks.[39]

In this sense, then, the term 'Islamophobia' is employed for its
perlocutionary effects;[40] that is, for the purpose of closing down
debate, and controlling what can and can't be said about Islam. In
part, this works because people self-censor for fear of provoking
Muslim ire. Malik, for example, recalls that he once began an essay on
Thomas Paine for the *Independent* newspaper by quoting from
Salman Rushdie's *The Satanic Verses*, only for the quote to be cut from
the final version because it was thought to be too offensive to
Muslims.[41] He remarks that the irony of censoring an essay written in
celebration of free thought seemed to escape the editor. More
recently, Random House cancelled the publication of *The Jewel of
Medina* – a novel that tells the story of Aisha, Muhammad's child
bride – after Denise Spellberg, an associate professor of Islamic
history at the University of Texas, complained that the book was a
'very ugly, stupid piece of work', which 'made fun of Muslims and
their history', and warned that there was a very real possibility that its
publication would provoke widespread violence.[42]

Spellberg's warning turned out to be accurate. On 4 September

2008, Gibson Square, a British publisher, announced that it had bought British and Commonwealth rights to the book. Just over three weeks later, the house of the owner of Gibson Square was firebombed, apparently as a protest against the publication of the book. Professor Spellberg, however, deserves no credit for her role in this affair, since if it had not been for her intervention, then likely Random House would have published the book, there would have been no fuss, and no firebomb.

It is understandable, if regrettable, that some Muslim organizations employ accusations of Islamophobia in an attempt to silence criticism of Islam and to shut down debate about their faith.[43] Religion is nothing if not partisan, and it would be naïve to expect religious believers to be appropriately restrained in defending their beliefs from criticism. However, what is more curious is that accusations of Islamophobia have become part of the political mainstream. As Malik puts it:

> Now everyone from Muslim leaders to anti-racist activists to government ministers want to convince us that Britain is in the grip of an irrational hatred of Islam ... Former Home Office Minister John Denham has warned of the 'cancer of Islamophobia' infecting the nation. The veteran anti-racist Richard Stone, who was a consultant to the Stephen Lawrence inquiry, suggests that Islamophobia is 'a challenge to us all'. The Director of Public Prosecutions has worried that the war on terror is 'alienating whole communities' in this country.[44]

The causes of all this handwringing are complex and could only be dealt with properly in a book length treatment. Nevertheless, it is worth pointing to a number of facets of the phenomenon. The first thing to say is that there is some old-fashioned religious apologetics going on here. There is a strong sense in which criticism of the beliefs and practices of one religion is a threat to the beliefs and practices of all religions. In particular, religious believers share a common interest in resisting the idea that the legal and moral legitimacy of their beliefs and practices is to be determined partly in relation to the demands of a secular value system (as we saw when we discussed the Cairo Declaration on Human Rights in Islam). Thus, for example, Rowan Williams, the Archbishop of Canterbury, has argued that Muslims should not have to choose between 'the stark alternative of cultural loyalty or state loyalty', and that it is dangerous simply to say that 'there's one law for everybody and that's all there is to be said, and anything else that commands your loyalty or allegiance is completely irrelevant in the processes of the court ...'[45]

> What we don't want I think is ... a stand-off where the law squares up to religious consciences over something like abortion or indeed by forcing a vote on some aspects of the Human Fertilisation and Embryology Bill in the commons as it were a secular discourse saying 'we have no room for conscientious objections' ...[46]

Needless to say, Williams has spoken out against Islamophobia, arguing that Western societies have to face up to what Islamophobia means:

> The Western World likes to think that it is inviting other cultures into a peaceful and enlightened atmosphere of civility. But the 'strangers' invited in may well be dismayed to discover that this peacefulness and enlightenment seems to include licence to express some very unpeaceful and unenlightened attitudes to minorities of various kinds. Just what kind of civility is this? the newcomer could ask.[47]

It is an unfortunate facet of even relatively secular Western societies that the ideas and beliefs of Williams, and his ilk, gain a public platform and are accorded a certain epistemological privilege simply by virtue of being informed by religious belief. Thus, for example, debates about the ethics of abortion, euthanasia, stem cell research, genetic engineering and sexual health tend to be poisoned by the fulminations of an endless parade of priests and the pious. The influence of religion in the institutions of political and civil society is reflected in the debate over Islamophobia. Not least, the various high-profile reports and analyses of the phenomenon that have appeared over the past decade tend to have been compiled by people who are themselves religious. For example, the Runnymede Trust report 'Islamophobia: A Challenge for Us All', was produced by a 'multi-religious' committee.[48] Its members included: Professor Akbar Ahmed, Chair of Islamic Studies at American University, Washington; Dr Zaki Badawi, then Principal of the Muslim College, London; Richard Chartres, the Bishop of London; Dr Philip Lewis, then an adviser on interfaith issues to the Bishop of Bradford; Rabbi Julia Neuberger; Hamid Qureshi, Chairman of the Lancashire Council of Mosques; Imam Abduljalil Sajid, chair of the Muslim Council for Religious and Racial Harmony; Dr Richard Stone, chair of the Jewish Council for Racial Equality; and Revd John Webber, then adviser on interfaith issues to the Bishop of Stepney.[49]

The committee responsible for 'Islamophobia: Issues, Challenges and Action', the Runnymede Trust's 2004 report, was also dominated by religious people. Moreover, the report acknowledges the 'substantial assistance' provided by a range of Muslim organizations, including the Muslim Council of Britain, and notes that comments on the report's final draft were received from Tahir Alam (Muslim Council of Britain); Mohammed Abdul Aziz (British Muslim Research Centre); Yahya Birt (Islamic Foundation); Inayat Bunglawala (Muslim Council of Britain); Khalida Khan and Humera Khan (An-Nisa Society); Iqbal Sacranie (Muslim Council of Britain); and Talha Wadee (then of the Lancashire Council of Mosques).

It would be easy to be lured into a polemical response to this kind of thing. Certainly there is something absurd about the idea that the best way to analyse anti-Muslim prejudice is to assemble a fairly random collection of religious apologists, all of whom have a vested interest in protecting religion from criticism, and many of whom have a specific interest in defending Islam, and then asking them to oversee a research project. After all, almost nobody would think that skinheads – however well educated and erudite – would be best placed to examine whether the far right is discriminated against, or that members of Fathers for Justice or Men's Aid should stand in judgement over whether the move towards sexual equality has gone too far. The point here is that it is almost impossible for people with vested interests to be objective about the issues that they're investigating. It seems highly unlikely that either of the Runnymede committees could *ever* have concluded that the problem of Islamophobia had been exaggerated (which is the view of Kenan Malik, for example).

Parenthetically, it is worth pointing out that it is not only the various studies of Islamophobia which have been flawed in this way. In the previous chapter, we noted that a recent British Home Office working group report on forced marriage denied that the practice had anything to do with religion. Moreover, it stated that 'describing forced marriage as a religious issue feeds prejudice and intolerance of other faiths' and that 'this misrepresentation of the nature of forced marriages should be challenged'. This is strong stuff, though as we saw when we discussed the issue earlier, the claim that forced marriage has nothing to do with religion is highly implausible. However, what's interesting here is the religious composition of the working group that produced the report: the overwhelming majority of its members were either Muslim, Hindu or Sikh, and it was co-chaired by two Muslim peers, Lord Ahmed of Rotherham and Baroness Uddin of Bethnal Green. The significant point about this is that it is inconceivable that the report was ever going to conclude anything other than that forced marriage is not a religious problem (moreover, it presumably explains why a statement as bizarre as 'No religion of the world restricts choice' appears in its pages).

The second general point worth making about the furore surrounding Islamophobia, certainly in Britain, is that it is partly fuelled by political manoeuvring and posturing, particularly on the part of a small, but vocal, group of ultra-leftists. This is a complex story, but in essence it has to do with a desire to exploit Muslim resentment – whether justified or otherwise – for political advantage. Nick Cohen explains as follows:

The far left had no future – that had been clear for decades. But if it could downplay its Marxism and appeal to Muslim grievance, maybe it could make it as a communalist party exploiting support for political Islam. Their theorists had been saying since the early Nineties that if they got into bed with Islam they could 'secretly try to win some of the young people who support it to a very different, independent, revolutionary socialist perspective'. Perhaps that daydream consoled them. Perhaps it allowed them to pretend to themselves that they were covertly building up the radical left rather than riding the Islamist tiger. Maybe they no longer believed in their hearts in 'independent revolutionary socialist perspectives' ... and just wanted to ally with the real threat to the established order.[50]

The theorist Cohen cites here is Chris Harman of the Socialist Workers Party, who set out a strategy for attracting young radicalized Muslims to the cause of revolutionary socialism in an essay he wrote in the mid-1990s. He claimed that

many of the individuals attracted to radical versions of Islamism can be influenced by socialists – provided socialists combine complete political independence from all forms of Islamism with a willingness to seize opportunities to draw individual Islamists into genuinely radical forms of struggle alongside them.[51]

Normally, there would be little chance of the Socialist Workers Party influencing anybody outside a small clique of unreconstructed Trotskyists and student radicals. However, the leading role that it played in the Stop the War Coalition increased its public profile, and brought it an influence far beyond its size or reputation. The party used the momentum generated by the anti-war mobilization to drive forward the launch of a new organization in January 2004 – 'Respect: The Unity Coalition'. According to Harman, Respect aimed to bring together the diverse forces of the anti-war movement, including revolutionaries, disillusioned Labour supporters, trade unionists, radical Muslim activists and people from the peace movement.[52]

Although the Respect project lasted only four years before falling apart in bitterness and recrimination, it quite successfully promulgated and popularized a discourse that links together the rhetoric of opposition to Islamophobia with anti-war sentiment and the politics of anti-imperialism. In the mid-1990s, Harman had insisted that it was the job of socialists to argue strongly with and to challenge Islamists, but the reality now is that the far left tends to see all criticism of Islam as being motivated by racism and imperialism. Thus, for example, Nahella Ashraf, chair of the Greater Manchester Stop the War Coalition, claims that:

> Islamophobia seems to be replacing anti-Semitism as the principal Western statement of bigotry against the 'other'. The pre-war Blackshirts attacked the newly arrived East End Jews, and today we have their modern equivalents going 'Paki-bashing'... 'Polite society' no longer has to worry about seeming racist, or sounding like the BNP, if they are talking about Muslims.[53]

Happily, the solution to the problem is simple:

> [T]here is one thing that is going to stop this growth in Islamophobia – that is to bring an end to George Bush's war on terror... This is just one of the reasons we must ensure that the Stop the War demonstrations are as big and as loud as possible.[54]

In similar vein, Rutgers University professor Deepa Kumar says about criticism of Islam that she is 'sick and tired of people who see themselves as part of the left writing articles that put a liberal gloss over what is, in essence, a right-wing "clash of civilizations" argument' and fed up that the anti-war movement in the USA, unlike its equivalent in Britain, has done 'nothing to defend Muslims against all the attacks they have faced both domestically and internationally'.[55] According to Kumar:

> The common thread that ties together all these attacks on Islam is a polarized view of the world. On one side are the values of freedom, democracy, rationality, women's rights, liberty, and civilization; all associated, furthermore, with Christianity. On the other side are a people

who are irrational, evil, barbaric, and uncivilized; who hate freedom and democracy and want to create, according to Bush, an Islamic empire stretching from Europe to South East Asia.[56]

These kinds of argument, although most common at the margins of the radical press, find expression in the mainstream media. The *Guardian*'s Seamus Milne, for example, has written a series of articles criticizing: 'anti-Islamist' crusaders; Muslims in the 'moderate Muslim business'; militant secularists who end up as apologists for Western supremacism and violence; 'relentless attacks' on Muslims, which are fuelled by the need to justify war in the Muslim world; and the demonization of Muslims by the 'political main-stream'.[57] In the USA, the pressure group FAIR (Fairness and Accuracy in Reporting) has recently published a report titled 'Smearcasting', which identifies 12 of the USA's 'leading Islamo-phobes' – the 'dirty dozen', as it puts it.

> The ... list includes some of the media's leading teachers of anti-Muslim bigotry, serving various roles in the Islamophobic movement. Some write the books that serve as intellectual fodder, others serve as promoters, others play the roles of provocateurs and rabble-rousers. Some ply their bigotry in the media's mainstream, others in the Internet's tributaries, while still others work talk radio's backwaters. Together with uncounted smaller players, they form a network that teaches Americans to see Islam in fearful terms and their Muslim neighbors as suspects.[58]

It's hard to know where to start with this sort of thing. Perhaps the first point to make is that the claim that the political mainstream in the West is seeking to demonize *all* Muslims in order to justify military operations in Iraq and Afghanistan is highly tenuous. Not least, George Bush, Tony Blair, John Howard, and even Dick Cheney, the *bête noire* of the anti-war left, have consistently made it clear that their quarrel is not with Islam, but with a particular 'distorted' or 'perverted' version of the religion, as practised by the kinds of people liable to fly aeroplanes into buildings.

- The world understands that we do not fight a religion. Ours is not a campaign against the Muslim faith ... this is a fight to save the civilized world and values common to the West, to Asia and to Islam. This is a struggle against evil, against an enemy that rejoices in the murder of innocent, unsuspecting human beings. That is why people in every part of the world and of all faiths stand together against this foe.[59] *Dick Cheney, 23 October 2001*
- All Americans must recognize that the face of terror is not the true ... face of Islam. Islam is a faith that brings comfort to a billion people around the world. It's a faith that has made brothers and sisters of every race. It's a faith based upon love, not hate.[60] *George Bush, 10 September 2002*
- Let me repeat what I have said before. This is not a struggle against Islam. It is a struggle against a perverted interpretation of Islam.[61] *John Howard, 4 October 2006*
- [L]et us remember that extremism is not the true voice of Islam. Millions of Muslims the world over want what all people want: to be free and for others to be free. They regard tolerance as a virtue and respect for the faith of others as a part of their own faith.[62] *Tony Blair, January/February 2007*

Of course, it is possible to argue that political leaders say one thing, but mean quite another: they might claim that there is no fight against Islam, and that Islam is respected as a religion of peace, but their actions demonstrate that they don't mean it. This is all well and good, but in this context irrelevant. The point is that Muslims are not *demonized* by the political mainstream in order to justify military action in the Middle East, or, for that matter, for any other reason. Or at least, if they are demonized, then it is so well disguised as to render it impotent as an ideological weapon. Even Karen Armstrong, the supreme apologist for Islam, has spoken in complimentary terms about the tone adopted in recent years by Western political leaders when talking about the religion.

Even more absurd is the accusation that criticism of Islam is necessarily, or as a matter of fact, racist in character. Of course, as we noted earlier, it is undeniable that criticism of Islam is sometimes motivated by racism, just as criticism of Zionism is sometimes motivated by anti-Semitism. However, it does not follow that all criticism of Islam is racist (any more than it follows that all criticism of Zionism is racist); that criticism of Islam is racist if its *consequence* is to increase anti-Arab or anti-Asian racism (any more than it follows that criticism of Zionism is racist if its consequence is to increase anti-Semitism); or that particular criticisms of Islam are necessarily false if motivated by racism (any more than it follows that particular criticisms of Zionism are necessarily false if motivated by anti-Semitism).

The arguments employed to support the contention that criticism of Islam is racist tend not to be well specified. They seem to depend on the following claims: 1) most Muslims in the West are Asian or Arab; 2) Asians and Arabs experience racism; 3) criticism of Islam both reflects racism and promotes racism; 4) it follows that criticism of Islam is racist. So, for example, in a rather confused article in *Socialist Worker*, Kevin Ovenden argues that anti-Asian racism has become 'fused with racist myths about followers of Islam', which derive from the rhetoric needed to justify imperialist intervention in the Middle East.[63]

In order to get clear about what is wrong with this kind of argument consider the following thought experiment. It's 1904 and King Leopold II of Belgium has been running the Congo as his own private company since 1876, with forced labour, mutilations, and a death toll estimated at ten million. The Catholic Church in Belgium has been a prolific source of propaganda in support of Leopold's 'civilizing mission' in the Congo. There is a significant minority Belgian Catholic population in Congo who are subject to a degree of racism, which sometimes takes the form of attacks on their Catholic beliefs. Most people in Congo deplore racist attacks on the Belgian minority population, saying that the issue is colonialist exploitation, not race, but many also consider the Catholic Church to be thoroughly complicit in the colonial enterprise, and want to say so loudly. They are aware that one consequence of doing so might be an increase in anti-Belgian racism, but they believe that the moral calculus comes out in favour of opposing the Catholic Church. They are also aware that they have a responsibility to ensure that their criticisms of Catholicism do not rely on pejorative stereotypes about Belgian ethnicity.

It seems clear that in this situation there is nothing necessarily racist about publicly disavowing the Catholic Church, even if the consequence is a rise in anti-Belgian racism. Likely most of us will make the judgement that if motives for criticizing the Catholic Church have nothing to do with ethnicity, and if criticisms are not couched in racial terms, then there is no racism. This judgement will probably hold even if the criticism amounts to the claim that Catholicism is barbaric, violent and irrational; and even if individual Catholics are held to be morally culpable for embracing what is taken to be a repugnant colonialist ideology.

This thought experiment shows that criticizing or condemning beliefs and practices that are in a particular context disproportionately associated with a specific ethnic group – in this case, Belgian Catholics – is not in and of itself racist. Whether it is or not depends upon motive, intent, whether ethnicity is invoked, and so on. It follows, therefore, that there is nothing inconsistent in criticizing Islam for being barbaric, irrational, primitive and sexist, while at the same time insisting that anti-Arab and anti-Asian racism is unacceptable and abhorrent.

There is a further worry here that is worth considering. It might be objected that while there is nothing necessarily racist in criticizing Islam, and while the right to criticize religion must be protected, it is nevertheless wrong to criticize Islam if the likely consequence is harm to some number of individual Muslims, perhaps, for example, as a result of a violent backlash against the religion. (The same of course can be said of criticism of any other religion and its adherents.) This is a complex issue, which will turn on how one views

Islam, consequentialist ethics, the notion of harm (whether or not 'offence' constitutes harm, for example), the limits of free speech, the value of religion, and so on. Although a full treatment is not possible here, because it would take another book, it is worth making a number of points.

The first is the obvious point that any moral calculus that depends on weighing up consequences might well come out in favour of criticizing Islam even if the result is harm to a large number of Muslims. The pertinent fact here is that the absence of criticism also has consequences, both in the narrow sense that it is almost inconceivable that religious practices such as FGM and child marriage will die away if they are not challenged, and also in the broader sense that there are disturbing implications for the existence and scope of free speech, which must be part of any moral calculus, if criticism is ruled out whenever it might cause harm.

The second thing to say is that how much harm one thinks is acceptable before it becomes necessary to rein back criticism of Islam will partly be determined by whether one judges the religion, and its associated beliefs and practices, to be irremediably malign. For example, if one has a strong, negative view of Islam, then one might judge that large amounts of harm are justified in the short-term if there is a reasonable expectation of undermining the religion, or certain of its practices, in the medium or long-term (this point also applies, of course, to religions other than Islam).

A third point, which is probably best approached via the earlier thought experiment about the Congo and Belgian colonialism, has to do with the complexities of moral culpability. If we ask the question how much harm to individual Belgians in the Congo is justified by the goal of resisting Belgian colonialism, it is likely that any response will be mediated by the fact that we normally consider people to be culpable for holding beliefs and values we take to be morally suspect. For example, if attacks on racists increase as a consequence of a concerted effort to stamp out racism, probably we will think that any harm suffered by racists counts for less in a moral calculus than it would if were we talking about an increase in attacks on non-racists. If this is the case, then it follows that how we balance the imperative to criticize Islam against the risk of harm to individual Muslims will partly depend on the extent to which we consider the beliefs and practices of Islam to be morally suspect and whether we consider individual Muslims to be culpable for embracing those beliefs and practices.

Obviously this point will be contentious so it is necessary to add a number of caveats. The claim here is *not* that Islam is morally equivalent to colonialism or racism. It is simply that we tend to think that people are culpable for holding malign beliefs and values, and that this will affect how we view the possibility that they might suffer harm as a consequence of their beliefs and values. This does not mean that such people deserve to suffer harm (though, somewhat ironically, this is the orthodox Islamic approach to apostates, for example), nor that we should not, all other things being equal, seek to minimize harm. However, it does mean – at least arguably – that when determining whether it is right to criticize a religion such as Islam, assuming we consider its beliefs and practices to be malign, the fact that its believers might be harmed as a result (perhaps because of a backlash against the religion) weighs less heavily than it would if we had judged the religion's beliefs and practices to be benign.

Of course it will be objected here that not all Muslims are committed to beliefs and values that any reasonable person would consider to be malign. Clearly this is true, though as we saw in Chapter 6 there are worries about the attitudes that many Muslims take towards issues such as homosexuality and Judaism. However, even if this is the case, it isn't clear that it gets the average Muslim believer entirely off the hook. There is the thought, however tentative, that it must be wrong to identify with a religion that is so overwhelmingly associated with patterns of misogyny. No doubt this line of argument is rebarbative, but it is not without merit. After all, it is a common thought that we should not align ourselves with institutions that are engaged in wrong-doing (particularly if we make no attempt to change them from within). Consider, for example, that many people who oppose what they take to be Western imperialism left those political parties that supported the invasion of Iraq in 2003 precisely because they felt that it would be unconscionable to remain within them. It is not obvious why this sort of reasoning does not also apply in the case of Islam, and indeed in the case of any other religion that is similarly misogynist (FLDS springs immediately to mind).

The final point to make about the worry that criticizing Islam might lead to harm to individual Muslims is that there is no requirement to see the moral issues raised by this possibility in purely consequentialist terms (though it is very difficult to escape consequentialist thinking entirely). It is quite possible to think that there is a moral imperative to criticize Islam for its misogynous aspects *even if* the harm that results outweighs any benefit. This is not as counterintuitive as it sounds. It is tied up with the thought that sometimes there is merit in resistance even if it is clear that to resist will be futile. Consider, for example, that the activists involved in the Civil Rights movement in the USA in the 1950s might have judged that the iniquities of racial discrimination justified their resistance even if they had known in advance that by resisting they were going to make things worse.

The same is true of the resistance during World War II, of abolitionists before and during the Civil War, of the people who struggled against colonialism in India and Africa and elsewhere, of the struggle against apartheid, of the people who flocked to Spain to resist Franco's coup, and so on. It is a common theme of such desperate struggles that safety and comfort are not enough, that great risks must be taken, that even if failure seems inevitable, the dice must be thrown. Sometimes even survival is not worth the price of putting up with injustice.

La Pasionaria said during the Spanish Civil War: 'I'd rather die on my feet than live on my knees.' (Ironic coming from a Stalinist, but never mind, the saying has resonance even if the sayer failed to understand it.) Just today (23 November 2008) we find, in a *Guardian*

article on the worsening situation for women and girls in
Afghanistan, a similar thought from an MP whose life is under
constant threat for the crime of defending women's rights.

> Talking at her home in central Kabul, she closed the living room door as
> her three young daughters played in the hall. 'You can't imagine what it
> feels like as a mother to leave the house each day and not know if you will
> come back again,' she said, her eyes welling up as she spoke.
> 'But there is no choice. I would rather die for the dignity of women than
> die for nothing. Should I stop my work because there is a chance I might
> be killed? I must go on, and if it happens it happens.'[64]

It is possible that the total sum of human happiness would, at
least temporarily, be increased if women like Shukria Barakzai gave
up, went back home, let themselves be silenced and stifled and
deprived of education and work and mobility and freedom. But
happiness isn't the only thing, happiness isn't enough. If happiness is
purchased at the price of degradation, subordination and rank
injustice, it becomes a sordid bargain.

There is a sense in which happiness isn't really what people want
– not exactly. We want something more complicated, more
demanding, more difficult; or even if we don't actually *want* anything
more than we want happiness, we may recognize – or passionately
insist – that there are higher, better values.

There is self-respect, for instance. There is dignity, which is often a
somewhat gassy bit of rhetoric but which also kicks off the Universal
Declaration of Human Rights and which at a minimum is the
antithesis of degradation and humiliation. People are often willing to
trade quite a lot of happiness for such a state.

There is justice, fairness, equality. There is the concept of human
rights, and all that it entails. There is the earth-shaking notion that
every human being deserves the same chance at a full, free, open life
as every other; that everyone deserves an education and the
opportunity to use it, and the ability to make choices about work,
family, and all the other ingredients of a flourishing life.

We want to be adults. We want to *be* adults, and we want to be *seen* as adults; we don't want to be coddled or protected or sheltered as if we were children. That means we have to take on the duties and responsibilities of adults. That doesn't necessarily lead to more happiness – it simply leads to a sense of being fully human, of participating in life, of doing what we can do and so ought to do.

There is also the question of time, and future generations. It could be, at any given moment, that a simple utilitarian or consequentialist calculation would come out on the side of quietism and the status quo. 'We're better off putting up with our situation than we would be if we fought back.' That often is a calculation that people have to make, and caution often does seem to tilt towards peace and survival and making the best of things. But that's true only as long as the calculation is confined to an eternal present. It is necessary to remember 1) that by submitting to injustice we are perpetuating injustice for the next generation and the generation after that and on into the future; and 2) that even if resistance makes things worse now, that doesn't mean it will make them worse forever. At the very least, the calculation becomes exorbitantly difficult to make; it no longer seems self-evident that the prudent course is to do nothing.

One of our operating assumptions in writing this book has been that systematic permanent institutionalized subordination is bad for people. This idea perhaps seems so self-evident to twenty-first-century Anglophones that there appears to be no need to argue it; it is perhaps one of the last remaining vestiges of the old faith in progress. Technology can wipe us out as well as save us; genocide keeps returning to inform us that moral progress is a bad joke; we solve old problems only to create new ones. But if you are a woman, or non-white, or gay, and you think back just a few decades, you may decide progress is not such a myth after all. Systematic subordination of most people used to be so taken for granted that it was largely invisible; that's no longer the case. Perhaps we are entitled to call that progress.

This is not necessarily because it makes the formerly subordinated more happy. It is more for other reasons. It is to do with being fully human, fully adult, fully part of human life lived in the real world. This may well be less comfortable, more work, more risky than being a subordinate – and yet at the same time fully worth the price.

8   Lipstick on a Pig

On 27 October 2008, a thousand spectators gathered in a stadium in Kismayu, Somalia to witness a 13-year-old girl being stoned to death by a group of more than fifty armed Islamist militiamen. Eyewitnesses stated that Aisha Ibrahim Duhulow was forced into a hole, buried up to her neck, and then pelted with stones until she died.[1] Amnesty International reported that at one point during the stoning, nurses were instructed to check whether Aisha was still alive. They removed her from the ground, declared that she was, and replaced her in the hole for the stoning to continue.[2]

Aisha was executed for 'adultery', but her aunt told the BBC that the teenager had in fact been raped by three armed men and that she took Aisha to the police station to report it. A few days later, after two suspects had been arrested, she was asked to return to the station with her niece; to her surprise the girl was arrested.

> 'I tried to speak to the police but they said they were not talking,' she said. Three days later, after Aisha had been tried in an Islamist court, she was stoned to death.
>
> 'They said that the girl had chatted up these men and had confessed to adultery … I don't know what crime she committed other than being raped; and I was not even allowed to see her body,' she said.[3]

A witness told the BBC's *Today* programme that the girl had been crying, pleading for her life, and had to be forced into a hole before the stoning.

'When she came out she said: "What do you want from me?"

'They said: "We will do what Allah has instructed us." She said: "I'm not going, I'm not going. Don't kill me, don't kill me."

'A few minutes later more than 50 men tried to stone her.'

The witness said people crowding round to see the execution said it was 'awful'.[4]

Awful indeed. A 13-year-old child buried up to her neck, awake, crying, pleading, and fifty grown men throwing stones at her head so that she will die in pain and terror. It's beyond awful – it's unendurable. It bespeaks a malfunction or absence of normal feelings that is scalding to contemplate. The men of the Islamist militia were not content simply to execute a young girl for being raped; they had to torture her to death, in front of an audience. They believed, or said they believed, that they were doing what Allah had instructed them to do – so they believed in, worshipped, and submitted to a god who wants young girls to be tortured to death.

This is not a new thought, of course, and it is not confined to Islam. Religion has long been soaked in the blood of those it deems heretical or impure. The Catholic Church specialized in religious brutality for a large part of its history, as Jean Calas, a French Calvinist who became a victim of a wave of anti-Protestantism, was shown in 1762. On the basis of no evidence, he was sentenced to death for the murder of his son, a crime putatively motivated by his desire to prevent his son from converting to Catholicism.

On 10 March of that year, he was strung up between two rings, and stretched until his four limbs came apart from their sockets. He did not die, and continued to protest his innocence, so he was subjected to the *question extraordinaire*, which involved water being poured into his mouth until his body swelled to twice its usual size. His torturers, still unable to extract a confession, then bound him to a scaffold, smashed his dislocated limbs, and left him to die. Two hours later, finding that he was still alive, they took 'pity' on him, and he was strangled until he was dead. So much for another of the great religions of peace. So much for Cherie Booth's claim that all religions 'share profound ideas on the dignity and special worth of each individual'.[5] So much for Karen Armstrong's claim that 'at the core of every single one of the world religions is the virtue of compassion'.[6]

The painful truth is that the intimate and inescapable connection that contemporary liberal believers like to see between God and love, theism and compassion, is largely a modern invention. It's far from universal now and it was vanishingly rare in the past. St Francis was an eccentric, not an exemplar. The Church placed Montaigne's *Essays* on the Index partly because he said, in 'On Cruelty', that

> even in the case of Justice itself, anything beyond the straightforward death penalty seems pure cruelty, and especially in us Christians who ought to be concerned to dispatch men's souls in a good state, which cannot be so when we have driven them to distraction and despair by unbearable tortures.[7]

The painful truth is that still, to this day, most people who believe in a god believe in a vindictive, punitive, even cruel god; a god who prefers some people to others and wants to see the others obliterated; a god who thinks women are greatly inferior to men and who thinks they should be harshly punished for the most trivial of reasons.

This god is variously thought to approve girls' being kept out of school and married off as children, murdered if they disobey, made pregnant before their bodies are ready, divorced at will, confined at home, deprived of resources, left destitute as widows, accused of being witches.

Most people who believe in a god believe in a god who authorizes all this, who in fact commands it. 'We will do what Allah has instructed us,' the militia said in Kismayu. Judith Shklar has this to say about the tension between opposing cruelty and obeying a god:

> To put cruelty first is to disregard the idea of sin as it is understood by revealed religion. Sins are transgressions of a divine rule and offenses against God ... However, cruelty ... is a wrong done entirely to *another creature*. When it is marked as the supreme evil it is judged so in and of

itself, and not because it signifies a denial of God or any other higher norm.[8]

There is a strong taboo on pointing out that there are no good reasons to believe in God, and an even stronger taboo on pointing out that the god of most religions is a cruel and unjust tyrant. It is not popular to suggest that humans seem to have a lasting taste for a god of revenge which they merely *label* a god of mercy. It is taken to be a violation of norms of 'respect' and 'tolerance' to say bluntly that the existing conceptions of God are mostly ones that endorse inequality, reasonless hatred, and many forms of xenophobia.

It is true, of course, that sometimes good things are done in the name of religion. There were religious motivations for opposing the slave trade (although that required ignoring many instructions in the Bible, New Testament[9] as well as Old), and no doubt people get something out of going to church once in a while (though if Will Herberg was right this is not so much about spiritual nourishment as fostering a sense of identity and belonging). Nevertheless, religion remains the last great prop and stay of arbitrary injustices and the coercion that backs them up. This is why there is so much danger in the widespread view that religion should be beyond criticism and that part of what it means when we say we 'respect' people is that we don't criticize their most cherished beliefs, especially – or perhaps only – if the beliefs are religious in nature.

Pragna Patel, of the secular feminist group Southall Black Sisters, noted in a 2008 article on religion and women's rights that

> Following the Rushdie Affair, the mood in all the various minority communities has been one of growing intolerance for all those who seek to challenge cultural and religious values and religious abuse of power.[10]

This is the trap of religion. Religion doesn't necessarily originate ideas about female subordination and male authority, but it does justify them; it does lend them a penumbra of righteousness, and it does make them 'sacred' and thus a matter for outrage if anyone disputes them. It does enable and assist and flatter moods of intolerance for all those who seek to challenge cultural and religious values and religious abuse of power. It does turn reformers and challengers into enemies of God.

Used in this way religion is like a matrix, a nutrient, a super-vitamin. It doesn't necessarily invent, but it amplifies, and nourishes, and protects. Religion is like the total body irradiation that destroys an immune system and lets an underlying infection take over. It's like a pesticide that destroys some insect species only to let others, freed from predators and competition, explode. It's like an antibiotic that kills some strains of bacteria only to help resistant strains thrive and flourish.

It's also a kind of protective colouring. There is no very compelling reason left to treat particular groups of people as inferior. It used to be possible (just barely) to think that human groups were literally and essentially different in some way profound enough to justify inequality, but it isn't possible any longer. All that's left is a literalist idea of God's will along with a conviction that God's will must not be disputed or disobeyed. Without that, a defence of unequal rights just looks like what it is – a frank defence of injustice. This puts religion in the uncomfortable position of being that which puts lipstick on a pig.

That is uncomfortable, but it is exactly the position religion is in. Religion, in the hands of the literalist defenders of God's putative will, is in the business of dressing up what would otherwise obviously be tired old prejudices and hatreds and plain exploitation, and making them seem vaguely respectable. Religion is the whited sepulchre, the warthog in a party dress, the dictator in a pink uniform plastered with medals, the executioner in white tie and tails.

It is possible to imagine a god who is a friend to the despised and downtrodden, a lover of fairness and equality and hope, a champion of rights and of our better natures. But that's not the God we have. It's a contingent fact but it is a fact that the God we have in the Big Three monotheisms is a god who originated in a period when male superiority was absolutely taken for granted. This God could have changed as human ideas about male superiority and female inferiority changed – and to some extent and in some sects, this God has changed – but on the whole, and especially in the more conservative religions, it hasn't. To a very large extent this is now what *defines* a religion as more or less conservative and/or fundamentalist. Unfortunately, indeed tragically, these religions are not the least popular ones in the world. They include most Catholicism, most Islam, Orthodox Judaism, and most Protestantism. Liberal Anglicanism, Unitarianism, Quakerism, Reform Judaism and rebelliously liberal branches of Catholicism and Islam don't add up to a very sizable minority; furthermore the numbers in liberal denominations are declining while those in illiberal denominations are skyrocketing.

The rigid God may be secretly kind and sympathetic in the victims' hearts, and let us hope it is, but in terms of the rules and laws and expectations, that God holds women in contempt. And *that* God, unfortunately, is the one who puts 'his' imprimatur on all those tyrannical laws. That is the God who makes cruelty holy and sacred and pious. That is the God who looks on approvingly when young girls are married off and raped, when women are whipped for showing a little hair, when men throw stones at a crying teenage girl until she is dead. That God is a product of history but taken to be eternal, which is a bad combination. That is the God who hates women. That God has to go.

Notes

Chapter 1

1. Omar Waraich, 'Five women beaten and buried alive in Pakistan "honour killing" ', *Independent*, 2 September 2008.
2. PakTribune, 1 September 2008, http://paktribune.com/news/index.shtml?205145, accessed 1 September 2008.
3. *Pakistan Post*, 1 September 2008, http://thepost.com.pk/EditorialNews.aspx?dtlid=180470&catid=10, accessed 1 September 2008.
4. Terri Judd, 'The Afghan women jailed for being victims of rape', *Independent*, 18 August 2008.
5. Jan Goodwin, *Price of Honor* (New York: Plume, 2003), p. 49.
6. Ibid., pp. 49–51.
7. Syed Shoaib Hasan, 'Strong feelings over Pakistan rape laws', BBC News, http://newsvote.bbc.co.uk/mpapps/pagetools/print/news.bbc.co.uk/2/hi/south_asia/6152520.stm, accessed 29 November 2008
8. Human Rights Watch, http://www.hrw.org/english/docs/2006/11/14/pakist14576.htm, accessed 29 November 2008.
9. Seth Mydans, 'In Pakistan, rape victims are the "criminals" ', *The New York Times*, 17 May 2002.
10. *Dawn*, 'Musharraf signs women's bill', 2 December 2006, http://www.dawn.com/2006/12/02/top7.htm, accessed 7 September 2008.
11. Women's International Network, 'Teenage mother sentenced to 180 lashes for childbearing', Winter 2001.
12. Ibid.
13. Human Rights Watch, 'Nigeria: Teenage Mother Whipped', 3 January

2001, http://hrw.org/english/docs/2001/01/23/nigeri212.htm, accessed 30 January 2008.

14. Amnesty International, 'The death penalty and women under the Nigeria penal systems', 10 February 2004, http://www.amnesty.org/en/library/asset/AFR44/001/2004/en/dom-AFR440012004en.html, accessed 22 June 2008.

15. Dan Isaacs, 'Living on Nigeria's death row', BBC News, 5 December 2001, http://news.bbc.co.uk/2/hi/africa/1694027.stm, accessed 29 November 2008.

16. CNN, 'Woman sentence to stoning freed', 23 February 2004, http://www.cnn.com/2003/WORLD/africa/09/25/nigeria.stoning/, accessed 22 June 2008.

17. *The Jerusalem Post*, 4 August 2008.

18. Ynet news, Israel, 14 August 2008, http://www.ynetnews.com/articles/0,7340,L-3582713,00.html, accessed 29 November 2008.

19. Daphna Berman, 'Woman beaten on J'lem bus for refusing to move to rear seat', *Ha'aretz*, 20 December 2006.

20. Goodwin, op. cit., p. 106.

21. Ibid., p. 107.

22. Barnaby Rogerson, 'Tariq Ramadan's act of piety', *The Times Literary Supplement,* 23 January 2008.

23. Franz Vanderpuye, 'Traditional beliefs cost women their freedom', Council for Secular Humanism, http://www.secularhumanism.org/library/aah/vanderpuye_8_3.htm, accessed 10 May 2007.

24. Sherry Amatenstein, *The New Jersey Star-Ledger*, 6 March 2006, http://www.rickross.com/reference/wicca/wicca51.html, accessed 10 May 2007.

25. Ibid.

26. Arpita Sutradhar, 'I witnessed a witch hunt in India', Orato.com, http://www.orato.com/node/392, accessed 7 March 2008.

27. Marilyn K. Angelucci, 'From chattel to freewomen: empowering India's females', November 2005, http://www.worldandi.com/subscribers/feature_detail.asp?num=24698, accessed 10 December 2007.

28. Ibid.

29. Uma Girish, 'India's outcast widows have new havens', 18 April 2004, http://www.womensenews.org/article.cfm/dyn/aid/1794/context/archive, accessed 11 December 2007.

30. Karijn Kakebeeke, 'Waiting for salvation', http://griefandrenewal.com/internat-moksha.htm, accessed 12 December 2007.

31. Arwa Damon, 'Shunned from society, widows flock to city to die', 5 July 2007, http://www.cnn.com/2007/WORLD/asiapcf/07/05/damon.india.widows/index.html, accessed 10 December 2007.

32. Ibid.

33. Jill McGivering, BBC News, 2 February 2002.

34. Ibid.

35. Celia Dugger, 'A refugee's body is intact but her family is torn', *The New York Times*, 11 September 1996.

36. Ibid.

37. Celia Dugger, 'U.S. grants asylum to woman fleeing genital mutilation rite', *The New York Times*, 14 June 1996.

38. Dugger, 'A refugee's body is intact but her family is torn', op. cit.

39. Ibid.

40. Christina Lamb, *The Times*, 13 November 2005, http://www.timesonline.co.uk/tol/news/world/article589698.ece, accessed 14 May 2007.

41. Ibid.

42. Human Rights Watch, press release 11 July 2006, http://hrw.org/english/docs/2006/07/06/afghan13700.htm, accessed 17 May 2007.

43. Shoib Najafizada, AFP, 14 May 2007.

44. Human Rights Watch, press release 11 July 2006, op. cit.

45. Carolyn Jessup, *Guardian*, 15 December 2007.

46. UN Population Fund, Campaign to End Fistula, http://www.endfistula.org/fistula_brief.htm, accessed 28 September 2008.

47. BBC News, 'They thought I was cursed', 19 October 2007, http://news.bbc.co.uk/2/hi/in_depth/7050934.stm, accessed 16 December 2007.

48. Sharon LaFraniere, 'Nightmare for African women: birthing injury and little help', *The New York Times*, 28 September 2005.

49. Ibid.

50. Andrew Buncombe, *Independent*, 13 October 2005.

51. Human Rights Watch, http://hrw.org/reports/2007/nicaragua1007/nicaragua1007web.pdf, accessed 15 December 2007.

52. Ibid., pp. 9–10.

53. Ibid., p. 13.

54. Human Rights Watch, 'Abortion: Chile', http://www.hrw.org/women/abortion/chile.html, accessed 23 June 2008.

55. Derek Scally, 'Polish girl caught up in row has abortion', *Irish Times*, 23 June 2008.

56. BBC News, 8 August 2000, http://news.bbc.co.uk/2/hi/africa/871032.stm, accessed 16 May 2007.

57. SBS World News, 18 May 2007, http://www.worldnewsaustralia.com.au/region.php?id=137084&region=6, accessed 18 May 2007.

58. Declan Walsh, *Guardian*, 12 April 2005, http://www.guardian.co.uk/pakistan/Story/0,2763,1457570,00.html, accessed 19 May 2007.

59. Steve Bird, 'Having fled Iraq, she died at the hands of her father', *The Times*, 12 June 2007.

60. David James Smith, 'Sins of the father', *The Times*, 11 November 2007.

61. Riazat Butt, ' "You're not my mother any more," shouted Samaira. Then her family killed her', *Guardian*, 15 July 2006.

62. BBC News, ' "Honour killing" brother jailed', 13 April 2006, http://news.bbc.co.uk/nolpda/ukfs_news/hi/newsid_4905000/4905758.stm, accessed 4 September 2008.

63. Ray Furlong, ' "Honour killing" shocks Germany', BBC News, 14 March 2005, accessed 5 September 2008.

64. BBC News, 'One in 10 "backs honour killings"', 4 September 2006, accessed 5 September 2008.

65. Centre for Social Cohesion, 'Islam on Campus', July 2008, http://www.socialcohesion.co.uk/pdf/IslamonCampusExecutiveSummary.pdf, accessed 5 September 2008.

66. BBC News, ' "Honour killings" law blocked', 8 September 2003, http://news.bbc.co.uk/2/hi/middle_east/3088828.stm, accessed 3 September 2008.

67. BBC News, 'Fresh "honour killing" in Jordan', 10 September 2003, http://news.bbc.co.uk/2/hi/middle_east/3097728.stm, accessed 3 September 2008.

68. Robert F. Worth, 'Tiny voices defy child marriage in Yemen', *The New York Times*, 29 June 2008.

69. Howard Schneider, 'Women in Egypt gain broader divorce rights', *The Washington Post*, 14 April 2000.

70. BBC News, 'Saudi women challenge driving ban', 18 September 2007,

http://news.bbc.co.uk/2/hi/middle_east/7000499.stm, accessed 3 September 2008.

71. Human Rights Watch, 'World Report 2002: Iran', http://www.hrw.org/wr2k2/mena3.html, accessed 3 September 2008.

72. AFP, 'Iran sentences women rights activists to jail', 3 September 2008, http://afp.google.com/article/ALeqM5hN0ONPqYRkJXLiJ-Smyrv1-PoY_dQ, accessed 3 September 2008.

Chapter 2

1. See, for example, http://news.bbc.co.uk/1/hi/world/middle_east/1867039.stm, accessed 23 November 2008. The cause of the blaze is contested. The official Saudi report claimed that it was caused by a discarded cigarette.

2. 'Mum's boyfriend braved horrific burns to try to save little Kyra', *Yorkshire Post*, 14 December 2007.

3. Again this is contested. Eyewitness statements do not seem to coincide with the findings of the official Saudi report. See, for example, http://news.bbc.co.uk/1/hi/world/middle_east/1893349.stm, accessed 23 November 2008.

4. Nourah Abdul Aziz Al-Kheriji, 'School tragedy: The lessons we adults forgot to learn', *Arab News*, 22 March 2002.

5. Mona Eltahawy, 'They died for lack of a headscarf', *The Washington Post* 19 March 2002 (http://www.library.cornell.edu/colldev/mideast/mutawsc.htm).

6. Khaled Abou El Fadl, 'The orphans of modernity and the clash of civilisations', *Global Dialogue*, 4, (2), Spring 2002, 1–16 (http://www.scholarofthehouse.org/orofmodandcl.html).

7. Cherie Booth, 'Women's human rights in the 21st Century', *BBC Today/Chatham House Lecture (2007)*, p. 7.

8. Ibid., p. 8.

9. George W. Bush, 'President's message for Eid al-Fitr', 13 December 2001, http://www.whitehouse.gov/infocus/ramadan/islam.html, accessed 23 November 2008.

10. Kofi Annan, 'Universal values of mercy, tolerance are at root of United

Nations search for global harmony, peace, says secretary-general at holy family church', 11 September 2006, http://www.un.org/News/Press/docs//2006/sgsm10630.doc.htm, accessed 23 November 2008.

11. Tony Blair, 'The duty to integrate: shared British values', *Downing Street Lecture*, 8 December 2006, http://www.policy-network.org/index.aspx?id=1160, accessed 23 November 2008.

12. Jean Chrétien, 'Notes for an address by Prime Minister Jean Chrétien on the occasion of a special House of Commons "Take Note" debate on the International Campaign against Terror', 15 October 2001.

13. Jacqui Smith, 'Our shared values: a shared responsibility', *First International Conference on Radicalisation and Political Violence*, http://press.homeoffice.gov.uk/Speeches/sp-hs-terrorism-keynote-jan-08, accessed 23 November 2008.

14. Stephen Law, *The Xmas Files* (London: Weidenfeld & Nicolson, 2003), p. 30.

15. Gen. 19.24–25 (which finds New Testament validation here: 2 Pet. 2.6).

16. 1 Sam. 6.19.

17. 1 Kgs 13.7–28 (incidentally, not the only death by lion in the Bible).

18. 2 Chron. 21.18–19.

19. Rom 2.7–8.

20. Karen Armstrong, *Muhammad: A Biography of the Prophet* (London: Phoenix Press, 2001), p. 15.

21. Karen Armstrong, *Islam: A Short History* (London: Phoenix Press, 2001), p. 13.

22. Ibid., p. 14.

23. Kecia Ali, *Sexual Ethics and Islam* (Oxford: Oneworld Publications, 2006), p. 137.

24. Armstrong, *Islam: A Short History*, op. cit., p. 13.

25. Armstrong, *Muhammad: A Biography of the Prophet*, op. cit., p. 157.

26. Reza Aslan, *No God but God* (London: Arrow Books, 2005), pp. 64–5.

27. Armstrong, *Islam: A Short History*, op. cit., p. 14. She repeats the identical claim in *Muhammad: A Biography of the Prophet*: 'Western critics often blame the Qur'an for its treatment of women, which they see as iniquitous, but in fact the emancipation of women was dear to the Prophet's heart.' (Armstrong, *Muhammad: A Biography of the Prophet*, op. cit., p. 191).

28. Armstrong, *Muhammad: A Biography of the Prophet*, op. cit., pp. 190–1.

29. Ibid., p. 191.

30. Ibid.

31. Armstrong, *Islam: A Short History*, op. cit., p. 14.

32. Armstrong, *Muhammad: A Biography of the Prophet*, op. cit., p. 191.

33. 'Frequently ...the other wives complained that he favoured Aisha. Muhammad tried to keep an impartial regime ...But he was only human and his real preference was clear to the whole *umma*.' (ibid., p. 202). See also Armstrong, *Islam: A Short History*, op. cit., p. 13.

34. Peter Lings, *Muhammad: His Life Based on the Earliest Sources* (Rochester: Inner Traditions, 2006), p. 286.

35. Armstrong, *Muhammad: A Biography of the Prophet*, op. cit., p. 236.

36. Ali, op. cit., p. 47.

37. For an analysis of wishful thinking, see Ophelia Benson and Jeremy Stangroom, *Why Truth Matters* (London: Continuum, 2006), pp. 107–34.

38. See Armstrong, *Muhammad: A Biography of the Prophet*, op. cit., p. 236.

39. Reza Aslan pursues a different tack here. He simply says that Mariyah was Muhammad's wife, which is hugely disingenuous (see Aslan, op. cit., p. 64). In some traditions, it is held that Muhammad married Mariyah, but she is normally accorded the status *umm walad* – a female slave who has borne a child to her master, and thereby becomes free on his death. See, for example, Tabari, *The History of al-Tabari, Volume VIII* (Albany: State University of New York Press, 1989), p. 58.

40. There is a layer of complexity here that is worth flagging up. It is arguable that the object of Muslim veneration is not so much the historical Muhammad as a symbolic Muhammad. Although this complicates the point about Prophetic example it does not negate it, since the historical Muhammad is part and parcel of any symbolic reconstruction.

41. Armstrong, *Muhammad: A Biography of the Prophet*, op. cit., p. 262. See also, for example, Karen Armstrong, *The History of God* (London: Vintage Books, 1999), p. 281.

42. See Lings, op. cit., p. 241.

43. See, for example, Ali, op. cit., pp. 39–40.

44. See, for example, Sahih Bukhari 59.459.

45. See Ali, op. cit., p. 43.
46. Koran 4.34 (translation by M. A. S. Abdel Haleem).
47. See Aslan, op. cit., pp. 69–70.
48. 'If a man invites his wife to sleep with him and she refuses to come to him, then the angels send their curses on her till morning.' (Sahih Bukhari 62.121) See also Sahih Muslim 08.3366, 08.3367, 08.3368.
49. Irshad Manji, *The Trouble with Islam Today* (Toronto: Vintage Books Canada, 2005), pp. 38–9.
50. See Koran 2.229; and Kecia Ali's discussion of 'triple talaq' (Ali, op. cit., pp. 25–7).
51. Karen Armstrong, *Muhammad: A Prophet for Our Time* (New York: HarperCollins, 2006), pp. 104–5.
52. Armstrong, *A Short History of Islam*, op. cit., p. 157.
53. Tabari, *The History of al-Tabari, Volume IX* (Albany: State University of New York Press, 1990), pp. 130–1.
54. Ibid., p. 131.
55. See Ali, op. cit., p. 144.
56. See Aslan, op. cit., pp. 64–5.
57. UNICEF Innocenti Research Centre, *Early Marriage, Child Spouses: Innocenti Digest No. 7*, March 2001, http://www.unicef.org/children-andislam/downloads/early_marriage_eng.pdf, accessed 12 July 2008.
58. *The New York Times*, 'Tiny voices defy child arriage in Yemen', 29 June 2008, http://www.nytimes.com/2008/06/29/world/middleeast/29marria-ge.html?_r=4&oref=slogin&pagewanted=print&oref=slogin&oref=slogin&oref=slogin, accessed 12 July 2008.

Chapter 3

1. John Stuart Mill, *The Subjection of Women*, Chapter 1.
2. FindLaw, http://caselaw.lp.findlaw.com/scripts/getcase.pl?court=US&vol=83&invol=130, accessed 17 August 2008.
3. The Council on Biblical Manhood & Womanhood, http://www.cbmw.org/About-Us, accessed 22 March 2008.
4. 'Core Beliefs: The Danvers Statement on Biblical Manhood and Womanhood', http://www.cbmw.org/Danvers, accessed 25 March 2008.

5. Patrick Henry College, 'Statement of Faith', http://www.phc.edu/about/faith.asp, accessed 17 August 2008.

6. Patrick Henry College, 'Statement of Biblical Worldview', http://www.phc.edu/about/BiblicalWorldview.asp, accessed 20 March 2008.

7. 'The Baptist Faith and Message', http://www.sbc.net/bfm/bfm2000.asp, accessed 19 January 2008.

8. Jimmy Carter, *Our Endangered Values* (New York: Simon and Schuster, 2005), p. 93.

9. Patricia Cohen, 'A woman's worth: 1857 letter echoes still; some basic disputes over feminism persist', *The New York Times*, 18 July 1998. (Katha Pollitt and Lynn Margulies were among the other contributors to this article.)

10. Gustav Niehbur, 'Southern Baptists declare wife should "submit" to her husband', *The New York Times*, 10 June 1998.

11. Catholic World News, 4 April 1997, http://www.cwnews.com/news/viewstory.cfm?recnum=4663, accessed 24 March 2008.

12. Australian Catholic Bishops Conference, 'Women's Contribution to the Life of the Church Celebrated on International Women's Day', 7 March 2008, http://www.acbc.catholic.org.au/org/opw/200803071662.htm, accessed 12 April 2008.

13. 'Apostolic Letter', *Mulieris Dignitatem*, http://www.vatican.va/holy_father/john_paul_ii/apost_letters/documents/hf_jp-ii_apl_15081988_mulieris-dignitatem_en.html, accessed 12 April 2008.

14. Ibid.

15. 'Letter of Pope John Paul II to Women', http://www.vatican.va/holy_father/john_paul_ii/letters/documents/hf_jp-ii_let_29061995_women_en.html, accessed 12 April 2008.

16. 'Letter to the Bishops of the Catholic Church on the Collaboration of Men and Women in the Church and in the World', http://www.vatican.va/roman_curia/congregations/cfaith/documents/rc_con_cfaith_doc_20040731_collaboration_en.html, accessed 21 August 2008.

17. Ibid.

18. Rosemary Ganley, 'Not much development in Rome on women', *Catholic New Times*, 12 September 2004.

19. Address of Pope Benedict XVI to convention on 'Woman and Man, the *Humanum* in its Entirety', 9 February 2008, http://www.vatican.va/

holy_father/benedict_xvi/speeches/2008/february/documents/hf_ben-xvi_spe_20080209_donna-uomo_en.html, accessed 12 April 2008.

20. Syed Hossein Nasr, *Ideals and Realities of Islam* (London: George Allen & Unwin, 1966), pp. 110–11. Quoted in Maryam Jameelah, 'The feminist movement and the Muslim woman', Islam 101, http://www.islam101.com/women/jameelah.htm, accessed 9 April 2008.
21. Ibid.
22. Ibid.
23. Ibid.
24. Neil MacFarqhar, 'For Muslim students, a debate on inclusion', *The New York Times*, 21 February 2008.
25. IslamOnline, http://www.islamonline.net/servlet/Satellite?pagename=IslamOnline-English-Ask_Scholar/FatwaE/FatwaE&cid=1119503549580, accessed 8 April 2008.
26. IslamOnline, http://www.islamonline.net/servlet/Satellite?cid=1119503549588&pagename=IslamOnline-English-Ask_Scholar/FatwaE/FatwaEAskTheScholar, accessed 8 April 2008.
27. Ibid.
28. IslamOnline, http://www.islamonline.net/servlet/Satellite?pagename=IslamOnline-English-Ask_Scholar/FatwaE/FatwaE&cid=1119503546384, accessed 8 April 2008
29. Mill, op. cit.
30. *USA Today*, 11 August 2007.
31. http://www.swbts.edu/index.cfm?pageid=676, accessed 27 March 2008.
32. Stephanie Simon, 'At Texas theological school: the role of the godly woman 101', *The Boston Globe*, 21 October 2007.
33. Ibid.
34. See Stephanie Coontz, *The Way We Never Were: American Families and the Nostalgia Trap*, (New York: Basic Books, 1992).
35. *Ordinatio Sacerdotalis*, 22 May 1994, http://www.vatican.va/holy_father/john_paul_ii/apost_letters/documents/hf_jp-ii_apl_22051994_ordinatio-sacerdotalis_en.html, accessed 2 April 2008.

Chapter 4

1. Carmen Bin Ladin, *Inside the Kingdom* (New York: Warner Books, 2004), p. 39.
2. Ibid., p. 56.
3. Ibid., p. 58.
4. Ibid., p. 60.
5. Ibid., p. 67.
6. Ibid., pp. 76–7, 79.
7. Ibid., p. 104.
8. Ibid., p. 105.
9. Ibid., p. 140.
10. Ibid., p. 147.
11. Human Rights Watch, 'Perpetual Minors: Human Rights Abuses Stemming from Male Guardianship and Sex in Saudi Arabia', 21 April 2008, http://hrw.org/reports/2008/saudiarabia0408/, accessed 13 September 2008.
12. See Amartya Sen, 'Missing women – revisited', *BMJ*, 327, 1297–1298, 6 December 2003.
13. As we saw in Chapter 2, the Koran helpfully makes this explicit, in Sura 2.223.
14. Tom Zoellner, 'Polygamy: throughout its history, Colorado City has been home for those who believe in virtues of plural marriage', *The Salt Lake Tribune*, 28 June 1998.
15. Stephen Lemons, *Phoenix New Times*, 21 April 2008, http://www.rickross.com/reference/polygamy/polygamy857.html, accessed 28 June 2008.
16. Wanted by the FBI, http://www.fbi.gov/wanted/fugitives/cac/jeffs_ws.htm, accessed 28 June 2008.
17. Brooke Adams, 'Polygamous teen bride', *The Salt Lake Tribune*, 14 September 2007.
18. Joseph Diaz, 'Elissa Wall on "What it was like to die" ', ABC News, 13 May 2008, accessed 28 June 2008.
19. Brooke Adams, 'Thou shalt obey', *The Salt Lake Tribune* 14 March 2004, http://www.religionnewsblog.com/6437/thou-shalt-obey, accessed 29 June 2008.
20. Ibid.

21. *The Salt Lake Tribune,* 'Specific duties and counsel to the mothers', 6 September 2007, http://www.sltrib.com/polygamy/ci_6819048, accessed 30 June 2008.
22. Ibid.
23. Ibid.
24. Matt Ridley, *The Red Queen* (New York: Penguin Books, 1995), p. 211.
25. 'My mother held me down', BBC News, 10 July 2007, http://news.bbc.co.uk/2/hi/health/6287926.stm, accessed 8 July 2008.
26. Martha Nussbaum, 'The feminist critique of liberalism', *Sex and Social Justice* (New York: Oxford University Press, 1999), p. 62.
27. Richard Shweder, 'When Cultures Collide: Which Rights? Whose Tradition of Values?', 2003, http://humdev.uchicago.edu/images/princetonfgmpaper.doc, accessed 9 July 2008.
28. Kenan Malik, 'Identity is that which is given', Butterflies and Wheels, http://www.butterfliesandwheels.com/articleprint.php?num=338, accessed 8 November 2008.
29. John Tierney, 'A new debate on female circumcision', TierneyLab, *The New York Times,* 30 November 2007, http://tierneylab.blogs.nytimes.com/2007/11/30/a-new-debate-on-female-circumcision/, accessed 10 July 2008.
30. Ayaan Hirsi Ali, *Infidel* (New York: Free Press, 2007), p. 32.
31. Afif Sarhan and Caroline Davies, 'My daughter deserved to die for falling in love', *Observer,* 11 May 2008.
32. Afif Sarhan and Caroline Davies, 'Mother who defied the killers is gunned down', *Observer,* 1 June 2008.
33. Ibid.
34. Ibid.

Chapter 5

1. 'Text of king's speech in Madrid, quoted by Saudi Gazette', Haj Information, http://www.hajinformation.com/main/y1937.htm, accessed 4 December 2008.
2. UNICEF, 'At a glance: Iran', http://www.unicef.org/infobycountry/iran.html, accessed 9 September 2008.

3. 'U.N. reports that Taliban is stockpiling opium', *The New York Times*, 27 November 2008, http://www.nytimes.com/2008/11/28/world/middleeast/28opium.html?ref=world, accessed 30 November 2008.

4. 'As if I Am Not Human: Abuses against Asian Domestic Workers in Saudi Arabia', Human Rights Watch, July 2008, http://hrw.org/reports/2008/saudiarabia0708/, accessed 19 July 2008.

5. Something, as Henri Tajfel showed, we hardly need encouragement to do.

6. 'Discussion of religious questions now banned at UN Human Rights Council', IHEU, 23 June 2008, http://www.iheu.org/node/3193, accessed 20 July 2008.

7. David Littman, 'Universal human rights and "human rights in Islam"', *Midstream*, February/March 1999.

8. Ibid.

9. Ibid.

10. Ibid.

11. Ibid.

12. 'The Universal Declaration of Human Rights' (henceforth UDHR), http://www.un.org/Overview/rights.html, accessed 28 September 2008.

13. 'Cairo Declaration on Human Rights in Islam' (henceforth CDHRI), http://www.unhcr.org/cgi-bin/texis/vtx/home/opendoc.htm?tbl=RSDLEGAL&page=research&id=3ae6b3822c, accessed 28 September 2008.

14. UDHR.

15. 'The Thailand Burma Railway', PBS, 26 June 2008, http://www.pbs.org/wnet/secrets/kwai/the-thailand-burma-railway, accessed 12 September 2008.

16. 20,000,000 people, 'Estimated war dead World War II', http://warchronicle.com/numbers/WWII/deaths.htm, accessed 28 September 2008, out of a population of between 162,000,000 and 193,077,000 in January 1939, Nation Master Encyclopaedia, http://www.nationmaster.com/encyclopedia/Demographics-of-the-Soviet-Union, accessed 28 September 2008.

17. UDHR.

18. CDHRI.

19. Ibid.

20. UDHR.

21. CDHRI.

22. Ibid.

23. Ibid.

24. Ibid.

25. Ibid.

26. Ibid.

27. Ibid.

28. Ibid.

29. Ibid.

30. BBC News, 'Afghan MPs back blasphemy death', 30 January 2008, http://
     news.bbc.co.uk/mobile/bbc_news/world/s._asia/721/72169/
     story7216976.shtml, accessed 9 September 2008.

31. Ibid.

32. Littman, op.cit.

33. Plato, *Euthyphro* 10a, Benjamin Jowett translation.

34. CDHRI.

35. *Christianity Today*, 30 May 2008, http://www.christiantoday.com/article/
     vatican.says.will.excommunicate.women.priests/19144.htm, accessed 12
     September 2008.

36. Pontifical Council for the Family, 'The Family and Human Rights', http://
     www.vatican.va/roman_curia/pontifical_councils/family/documents/
     rc_pc_family_doc_20001115_family-human-rights_en.html, accessed 6
     August 2008.

37. http://www.wfdd.org.uk/united_nations/UNHRtsCommissT_ext.pdf,
     accessed 4 December 2008.

38. International Humanist and Ethical Union, 'How the Islamic states
     dominate the UN Human Rights Council', 2 April 2007, http://
     www.iheu.org/node/2546, accessed 10 August 2008.

39. Luiza Savage, 'Stifling free speech – globally', *MacLean's*, 23 July 2008,
     http://www.macleans.ca/world/global/article.jsp?con-
     tent=20080723_27859_27859&page=3, accessed August 10 2008.

Chapter 6

1.   Home Office (HO), 'A Choice by Right: The Report of the Working Group
     on Forced Marriage', June 2000.

2. Foreign and Commonwealth Office (FCO), 'Young People and Vulnerable People Facing Forced Marriage: Practice Guidance for Social Workers', March 2004.

3. House of Commons (HC), vol. 463, col 647, 27 July 2007.

4. 'Fears for 2000 "missing pupils" ', BBC News, http://news.bbc.co.uk/1/hi/uk/7290374.stm, accessed 29 August 2008.

5. 'Forced marriage', BBC Religion and Ethics, http://www.bbc.co.uk/ethics/forcedmarriage/introduction.shtml, accessed 29 August 2008.

6. Nazia Khanum, 'Forced marriage, family cohesion and community engagement', Equality in Diversity, 2008, pp. 20–1.

7. FCO, op. cit., p. 2.

8. Janice Boddy, 'Womb as oasis: the symbolic context of Pharaonic circumcision in rural northern Sudan', *American Ethnologist*, 9, (2), 1982, 695–6.

9. Carla Obermeyer, 'Female genital surgeries: the known, the unknown, and the unknowable', *Medical Anthropology Quarterly* 13, (1), 1999, 88.

10. See Herodotus, *Histories*, 2.104.

11. Strabo, *Geographica*, Book 17, Chapter 2.

12. See, for example, Hanny Lightfoot-Klein, *Prisoners of Ritual: An Odyssey Into Female Genital Circumcision in Africa* (Binghamton: Haworth Press, 1989), p. 88.

13. Here is Matthias S. Klein on the origin of FGM: 'Most likely having originated in the Nile valley and then spread to sub-Saharan Africa (and in the case of the Kurds also to some communities further the east), over time FGM was integrated into whatever new religion came along – including Islam, Christianity, and Judaism (in the case of the Ethiopian Jews).' ('Stemming the bloody tide', guardian.co.uk, http://www.guardian.-co.uk/commentisfree/2008/jun/21/egypt.fgm, accessed 31 August 2008.) Alison Slack, however, has a different view: 'The cultural and geographical origins of the practice are unknown. The incidence is, however, so geographically dispersed and occurs among such a variety of cultures that it is reasonable to assume that the practice arose independently among different groups of people.' (Alison Slack, 'Female circumcision: a critical appraisal', *Human Rights Quarterly*, 10, (4), 1988, 443.

14. Muhammad Salim al-Awwa, 'Neither a *Sunna*, nor a sign of respect', http://www.emro.who.int/publications/EMROPublications/HealthEd

Religion/CircumcisionEn/EMRO%20Pub-Hlth%20Ed.%20thru%20Relig-circ-FECI.htm, accessed 5 September 2008.

15. Ibid.

16. Cited in Sami Aldeeb, 'Male and female circumcision: the myth of the difference' in Rogaia Mustafa Abusharaf, *Female Circumcision: Multicultural Perspectives* (Philadelphia: University of Pennsylvannia Press, 2006), p. 59.

17. Yusuf al-Qaradawi, 'Circumcision: juristic, medical & social perspectives', Islam Online, 13 December 2004, http://www.islamonline.net/servlet/Satellite?pagename=IslamOnline-English-Ask_Scholar/FatwaE/FatwaE&cid=1119503548446, accessed 7 September 2008.

18. Aldeeb, op. cit., p. 59.

19. UNICEF, 'Female Genital Mutilation/Cutting: A Statistical Exploration', 2005, p. 10.

20. We are assuming here – correctly! – that animism and other traditional beliefs do not count as non-belief.

21. Rachel Reid, 'Making a public splash in Saudi', BBC Online, 5 May 2007, http://news.bbc.co.uk/1/hi/programmes/from_our_own_correspondent/6625393.stm, accessed 18 September 2008.

22. The Pew Global Attitudes Project, 'Unfavorable Views of Jews and Muslims on the Increase in Europe', 17 September 2008, p. 18, http://pewglobal.org/reports/pdf/262.pdf, accessed 18 September 2008.

23. Ibid., pp. 23–4.

24. The Pew Global Attitudes Project, 'Among Wealthy Nations … U.S. Stands Alone in its Embrace of Religion', 19 December 2002, http://pewglobal.org/reports/display.php?ReportID=167, accessed 18 September 2008.

25. Magali Rheault and Dalia Mogahed, 'Iranians, Egyptians, Turks: Contrasting Views on Sharia', 10 July 2008, http://www.gallup.com/poll/108724/Iranians-Egyptians-Turks-Contrasting-Views-Sharia.aspx, accessed 18 September 2008.

26. The Pew Global Attitudes Project, 'Muslims in Europe: Economic Worries Top Concerns about Religious and Cultural Identity', 6 July 2006, http://pewglobal.org/reports/display.php?ReportID=254, accessed 18 September 2008.

27. The Pew Global Attitudes Project, 'World Publics Welcome Global Trade – But Not Immigration', 4 October 2007, p. 34, http://pewglobal.org/reports/pdf/258.pdf, accessed 18 September 2008.

28. Magali Rheault and Dalia Mogahed, 'Moral Issues Divide Westerners From Muslims in the West', 23 May 2008, http://www.gallup.com/poll/107512/Moral-Issues-Divide-Westerners-From-Muslims-West.aspx, accessed 18 September 2008.
29. The Pew Global Attitudes Project, 'Unfavorable Views of Jews and Muslims on the Increase in Europe', op. cit., p. 10.
30. Ibid.
31. The Pew Global Attitudes Project, 'World Publics Welcome Global Trade – But Not Immigration', op. cit., p. 35.
32. Ayaan Hirsi Ali, *Infidel* (New York: Free Press, 2007), pp. 30–1.
33. U.S. Department of State, 'Mali: Report on Female Genital Mutilation (FGM) or Female Genital Cutting (FGC)', 1 June 2001, http://www.state.gov/g/wi/rls/rep/crfgm/10105.htm, accessed 20 September 2008.
34. The way that Max Weber uses the expression 'elective affinity' is best illustrated by a quote from his *Protestant Ethic and the Spirit of Capitalism*: 'in view of the immense confusion of reciprocal influences between the material bases, the forms of social and political organization, and the intellectual and spiritual contents of the cultural epochs of the Reformation, one can proceed only by first of all inquiring as to whether and in what points definite elective affinities between certain forms of its religious faith and its work ethic are discernible. Thereby and at the same time, the manner and the general direction in which in consequence of such elective affinities the religious movement affected the development of the material culture will be clarified as much as possible'. (Max Weber, *The Protestant Ethic and the Spirit of Capitalism* (New York: Scribners, 1958, pp. 91–2)).

Chapter 7

1. The Runnymede Trust, 'Islamophobia: A Challenge for Us All – Summary', 1997, http://www.runnymedetrust.org/uploads/publications/pdfs/islamophobia.pdf, accessed 25 September 2008.
2. Anthony Grayling, 'Believers are away with the fairies', *Daily Telegraph*, 26 March 2007, http://www.telegraph.co.uk/portal/main.jhtml?view=DETAILS&grid=A1YourView&xml=/portal/2007/03/26/nosplit/ftreligion126.xml, accessed 25 September 2008.

3. 53% of Egyptian Muslims think that suicide bombings can be justified; 54% of Jordanian Muslims agree; as do 50% of Lebanese Muslims, and 44% of Nigerian Muslims. (The Pew Global Attitudes Project, 'Unfavorable Views of Jews and Muslims on the Increase in Europe', 17 September 2008, p. 25, http://pewglobal.org/reports/pdf/262.pdf, accessed 18 September 2008.)

4. Ibid., p. 29.

5. Kenan Malik, 'The Islamophobia myth', http://www.kenanmalik.com/essays/islamophobia_prospect.html, accessed 28 September 2008.

6. The philosopher J. L. Austin distinguished between the conventional meaning of a speech act – in his terms, the locutionary act – and the *effect* of a speech act, what he called the perlocutionary act or perlocutionary effect.

7. Malik, op. cit.

8. See, for example, Asra A. Nomani, 'You still can't write about Muhammad', *The Wall Street Journal*, 6 August 2008, http://online.wsj.com/article/SB121797979078815073.html, accessed 29 September 2008.

9. This is not the whole story, of course. Yasmin Alibhai Brown points out that the idea of Islamophobia is sometimes used to explain away Muslim underachievement. 'By and large the lowest achieving community in this country whether we're talking about schools, Universities, occupations, professions and so on are by and large, the majority are Muslims. When you talk to people about why this is happening the one reason they give you, the only reason is Islamophobia. Uh uh. It is not Islamophobia that makes parents take 14 year old bright girls out of school to marry illiterate men, and the girl has again to bring up the next generation who will again be denied not just education but the value of education. What Islamophobia does is it just becomes a convenient label, a figleaf, a reason that is so comfortable for Muslims whenever they have to look at why they aren't in the places that they have to be.' Cited in the transcript of Kenan Malik's television programme, *Are Muslims Hated?*, http://www.kenanmalik.com/tv/c4_islamophobia.html, accessed 5 October 2008.

10. Malik, 'The Islamophobia myth', op. cit.

11. See 'Sharia law in the UK is "unavoidable" ', BBC News, 7 February 2008, http://news.bbc.co.uk/1/hi/uk/7232661.stm, accessed 5 October 2008.

12. 'BBC Interview – Radio 4 World at One', 7 February 2008, http://www.archbishopofcanterbury.org/1573, accessed 5 October 2008.
13. Rowan Williams, 'Mansion House Speech: Antidote to Blasphemy v. Free Speech Arguments is Respect and Civility', 7 February 2006, http://www.archbishopofcanterbury.org/312, accessed 5 October 2008.
14. The Runnymede Trust, 'Islamophobia: A Challenge for Us All', op. cit.
15. Ibid.
16. Nick Cohen, *What's Left: How Liberals Lost Their Way* (London: Fourth Estate, 2007), p. 309.
17. Chris Harman, 'The Prophet and the proletariat', *International Socialism*, 64, Autumn 1994, http://pubs.socialistreviewindex.org.uk/isj64/harman.htm, accessed 29 October 2008.
18. Chris Harman, 'The crisis in Respect', *International Socialism*, 117, December 2007, http://www.isj.org.uk/?id=396, accessed 30 October 2008.
19. Nahellah Asraf, 'Islamophobia: resisting prejudice', Socialist Worker Online, 5 February 2008, http://www.socialistworker.co.uk/art.php?id=14110, accessed 1 November 2008.
20. Ibid.
21. Deepa Kumar, 'Danish cartoons: racism has no place on the left', MR Zine, 12 February 2006, http://mrzine.monthlyreview.org/kumar210206.html, accessed 1 November 2008.
22. Deepa Kumar, 'Islam and Islamophobia', *International Socialist Review*, 52, March–April 2007, http://www.isreview.org/issues/52/islamophobia.shtml, accessed 2 November 2008.
23. See http://www.guardian.co.uk/profile/seumasmilne, accessed 1 December 2008.
24. FAIR, 'Smearcasting: How Islamophobes spread fear, bigotry and misinformation', October 2008, p. 8, http://www.smearcasting.com/pdf/FAIR_Smearcasting_Final.pdf, accessed 3 November 2008.
25. Dick Cheney, 23 October 2001, http://www.whitehouse.gov/vicepresident/news-speeches/speeches/vp20011023.html, accessed 4 November 2008.
26. See http://www.whitehouse.gov/infocus/ramadan/islam.html, accessed 4 November 2008.
27. See http://www.theaustralian.news.com.au/story/0,20867,20520355-601,00.html, accessed 4 November 2008.

28. Tony Blair, 'A battle for global values', *Foreign Affairs*, January/February 2007, p. 5, http://www.foreignaffairs.org/20070101faessay86106-p40/tony-blair/a-battle-for-global-values.html, accessed 4 November 2008.

29. Kevin Ovenden, 'Islam and racism', *Socialist Worker*, 1910, 17 July 2004, http://www.socialistworker.co.uk/art.php?id=907, accessed 5 November 2008.

30. Clancy Chassay, 'Acid attacks and rape: growing threat to women who oppose traditional order', *Guardian*, 23 November 2008, http://www.guardian.co.uk/world/2008/nov/22/afghanistan-gender-women-taliban, accessed 24 November 2008.

Chapter 8

1. 'Stoning victim "begged for mercy"', BBC News, 4 November 2008, http://news.bbc.co.uk/2/hi/africa/7708169.stm, accessed 1 December 2008.

2. Amnesty International, 31 October 2008, http://www.amnesty.org/en/news-and-updates/news/child-of+-13-stoned-to-death-in-somalia-20081031, accessed 1 December 2008.

3. 'Somalis grow fearful of Islamists', BBC News, 12 November 2008, http://news.bbc.co.uk/2/hi/africa/7722701.stm, accessed 1 December 2008.

4. 'Stoning victim "begged for mercy"', op. cit.

5. See Chapter 2.

6. Karen Armstrong, 'Why is the charter for compassion so important?', *The Huffington Post*, 18 November 2008, http://www.huffingtonpost.com/karen-armstrong/why-is-the-charter-for-co_b_144666.html, accessed 3 December 2008.

7. Michel de Montaigne, *The Complete Essays*, translated by M. A. Screech (London: Penguin Books, 1993), p. 482.

8. Judith Shklar, 'Putting cruelty first', *Ordinary Vices* (Cambridge, MA: Harvard University Press, 1984), pp. 8–9.

9. 1 Pet. 2.1819 to name just one.

10. Pragna Patel, 'Faith in the state? Asian women's struggles for human rights in the U.K.', *Feminist Legal Studies*, April 2008, 7.

Index

abortion
  banning of 21–4
Afghanistan 2, 9, 10, 16–19, 107–8
Ali, Kecia 38
  on Koran and divorce 46
  on Prophet Muhammad
    as exemplary 38
    marriage to Aisha 38
      age of Aisha at
        consummation 48
    'relationship' with Mariyah the
      Copt 43
Armstrong, Karen 36–51, 164
  absence of references 47
  OK Magazine style 39
  on concubinage and polygamy
    motivated by concern for
    women 41–2
  on Islam as religion of peace 36–7
  on progressive Koran 41
  on Prophet Muhammad 37–51
    as feminist 37
    marriage to Aisha 37–44, 46–51
      age of Aisha at
        consummation 47–9
    'relationship' with Mariyah the
      Copt 42–4
  silence about inconvenient facts
    44–6
  style of apologetics 40–2, 43–6, 47
  guilty of wishful thinking 43
  writings on Islam as exercise in

caricature 51
Aslan, Reza 45
  on Prophet Muhammad
    marriage to Aisha 39–40, 49

benign religion (putative) 34–6, 131
  Annan, Kofi on 34
  Blair, Tony on 34
  Booth, Cherie on 33–4
  Bush, George W. on 34
  standard defence of claim 35–6,
    131

Cairo Declaration of Human Rights in
    Islam 114–27
  compared to Universal Declaration
    of Human Rights 115–19,
    121–3
  lacking clarity121–3
  on marriage 118
  rights conditional upon Sharia 117,
    120–4
  its standing 123–5
  not universal 115–27, 122–4
Catholic Church 60–5, 79–81, 127–9
child marriage 20–1, 28–9, 93–4
  and Prophet Muhammad's marriage
    to Aisha 50–1
culture and religion 132–50
  and female genital mutilation
    134–50
  and forced marriage 132–3

culture and religion *cont.*
    impossibility of pulling culture and
        religion apart from one
        another 150
    religion as omnipresent social
        force 144–8

'defamation' of religion 129–30

education
    Cairo Declaration of Human Rights in
        Islam on 119
    restrictions on 11–12, 17–19, 76–8,
        88, 91

female genital mutilation 14–16,
        98–104, 134–50
    Ayaan Hirsi Ali's experience 103–4
    American Anthropological
        Association's hand
        wringing 102
    approved of by some Islamic
        scholars 138–9
    causally bound up with beliefs and
        values that necessarily have a
        religious dimension 148–50
    claim that it is not linked to
        religion 134–6
        empirical evidence for this claim
            not conclusive 136–42
    and death 14–15
    debate over terminology 103–4
    demographics of practice 139–41
        difficulty of establishing causal link
            between religion and
            FGM 141–2
    forced 15–16
    history of practice 134–5, 136
    justifications offered for 16, 99
    opponents of campaigns to
        eradicate FGM 98–9
    and pain 14, 16
    support for in sacred texts of
        Islam 137–9
fistula 20–1
flogging 3, 5, 6, 8, 9, 12

forced marriage 18, 19–20, 26, 131–4
    claim that it has nothing to do with
        religion 131–2
    incoherence of this claim 132–3
Fundamentalist Church of Latter Day
    Saints 19–20, 93–8

groupthink *see* reification of groups/
    community

honour killing 1, 25–8, 89, 104–7
    and the law 28
    support for 27

India 12
    and widows 13–14
Intermediate Girls' School No. 31,
    Mecca 31–3
    fire at 31–3
    and religious police 32–3
    reaction of commentators to
        32–3
Iran 8–9, 24, 108
    child marriage 51
Iraq 104–107
Islam 31–51, 66–72, 86–92, 98–107,
    111–27, 131–72
Islamophobia 151–72
    absurdity of claiming criticism of
        Islam is necessarily
        racist 164–6
    accusation of Islamophobia
        employed for political
        ends 160–3
    accusation of Islamophobia
        employed to defend
        religion 152, 157–60
    criticism of Islam might encourage
        racism 166–8
    defined 152–3
        definition badly flawed 153–5
    Islam not a homogenous entity 152,
        155
    resistance to Islam does not
        necessarily require a utilitarian
        justification 169–72.

Law, Stephen
  God as mafia boss 34–5

marriage 1, 18, 26
  Cairo Declaration of Human Rights in
    Islam on 118
  Prophet Muhammad's marriage to
    Aisha 37–44, 46–51
  and sexual division of labour 56–82
modesty
  and 'modesty police' 7–8
  and Saudi Arabia 86–90
  and veiling 8–9
multiculturalism 101–2

Nigeria 5–7, 21
  Zamfara 5–7, 9, 24

Pakistan 1, 2–5, 24–5
  Hudood Ordinance 3–4, 10
polygamy 19–20, 41–2, 88
  and Fundamentalist Church of Latter
    Day Saints 19–20, 93–8

rape 2–5
  victim as criminal 2, 3–5
reification of groups/community
    100–2
  community loyalty 110–11
    dangers of 112–13
    and epistemology 110–11
  and 'defamation' of religion 130
  erroneous presumption of
    unanimity 101
  and Vatican's 'Charter of the Rights of
    the Family' 128–9
religion prevents people from being
    fully human 170–2
religious violence 1–30, 172–5

Saudi Arabia 29
  abuse of domestic servants in 109
  Carmen Bin Laden's story 86–90
  fire at Intermediate School
    No. 31 31–3
  King Abdullah says 'mankind'

    suffering from loss of
    values 108–10
Sewing Circles of Herat 17–18
  and Lamb, Christina 17
sexual division of labour 52–82, 86
  Myra Bradwell case 55
  and Cairo Declaration of Human
    Rights in Islam 119
  Catholic Church's view 61–6
    women excluded from religious
      leadership 78–82
      weakness of justifications
        for 80–2
  and 'complementary difference'
    54–5, 68, 70–2
    John Stuart Mill on 74–5
    not a persuasive view 72–4
  The Council on Biblical Manhood
    and Womanhood 55–7
    advocates male superiority and
      female subordination 56–7
  Fundamentalist Church of Latter Day
    Saints 97
  Islam's approach 66–72
    'complementary difference' 68,
      70
    man or father as Imam 66–8
    women excluded from religious
      leadership 68–70
  John Stuart Mill on 52–3
  Patrick Henry College
    Statement of Faith 57–8
  reflected in religious education
    Southwestern Baptist Theological
      Seminary 76–8
  religion as justification for 54–82,
    176–7
  Southern Baptist Convention
    wife must submit to husband
      58–60
sexuality 83–107
  control of female sexuality 83–107
    Carmen Bin Laden's
      experience 86–90
      annihilation of female
        personality 89

sexuality, *cont.*
    everything is forbidden or
        shameful 87
    segregated education 88
    a wife's fear of her husband 88
    female genital mutilation 98–104
    ferocious control 90–2
    Fundamentalist Church of Latter
        Day Saints 93–8
    absolute obedience
        required 94–5
    and 'willing submission' 97
    woman worth a fraction of
        man 95–6
    women 'given to' men 96
    and honour killing 104–7
    woman as 'danger magnet' 83–6
    women's genitals as 'natural
        resource' 93–7
Sharia 3–7, 10
    and evidence 5–7
    and punishment 3, 5–7, 8, 9
Somalia 98
    stoning 172–4
    Southern Baptism 58–60, 76–8
Southern Baptist Convention 58–60
    espouses a sexual division of
        labour 58–60
stoning 7, 172–4

Taliban 10, 16–19, 107–8

United Nations Human Rights Council
    and 'defamation' of religion
        129–30
    meeting on 16 June 2008 111–12
United States of America 19–20, 55–60
    Fundamentalist Latter Day
        Saints 93–8
Universal Declaration of Human
        Rights 113–27
    and Cairo Declaration of Human
        Rights in Islam 114–27
    Islamic objections to 113–14

Vatican's 'Charter of the Rights of the
        Family' 127–9
vindictive God 175–8

whipping *see* flogging
widows 13–14
witchcraft 11–12

Yemen 28–9
    and child marriage 50–1
        Muhammad's marriage to Aisha as
            justification for 51

zina (adultery) 3–7